# A Time for Sorrow

FROM THE LIBRARY OF
THE INSTITUTE FOR
WORSHIP STUDIES
FLORIDA CAMPUS

"As the contributors to *A Time for Sorrow* so helpfully demonstrate, the practice of lament has always constituted a profound expression of faith. The failure of contemporary Christianity to adopt the language of lament robs the church of one of its greatest resources. In an age where the pursuit of happiness is prized above all, *A Time of Sorrow* offers a different path, where joy and sorrow are not competitors but essential expressions of a robust faith."

—Kit Barker, Lecturer in Old Testament
Sydney Missionary and Bible College, Australia

"Joining the invitation to explore lament through this book will undoubtedly expand the reader's appreciation of the importance of practicing lament for both individuals and communities of faith. Through considering what the biblical text, theology, history, and contemporary pastoral practice have to contribute to our understanding of this vital subject, these writers insightfully reflect on a challenging and yet necessary practice. In their own unique ways, each contributor reminds us that God is not detached from our need to lament and, in fact, empathizes with us, listening and responding to our distress. They also remind us that the biblical text of both testaments describes and models lament for attentive readers to appreciate and take as exemplary when responding to their own distresses. There is much here to be reflected upon and heeded in our practice of lament within the church and beyond."

—David Cohen, Head of Biblical Studies
Lecturer, Hebrew Bible and Language
Vose Seminary, Bentley, Australia

"The recent upsurge in works that explore Christian appropriation of Old Testament lament has been much needed. For too long, the Western church has neglected the topic and assumed a dominant narrative of power and success. Utilizing interdisciplinary insights from seasoned scholars, *A Time for Sorrow* challenges that assumption and offers an alternative biblical, theological, and pastoral response to the reality of pain and suffering. Truth be told, we need more books like this. Left unaware of the power of lament, the church is left to groan in silence. How welcome, then, to find a book that encourages God's people to cry out to him as a means of remaining faithful till the day Christ appears."

—G. Geoffrey Harper, Lecturer in Old Testament
Sydney Missionary and Bible College, Australia

"*A Time for Sorrow: Recovering the Practice of Lament in the Life of the Church* is a book that truly lives up to its title. Integrating excellent scholarship, keen theological reasoning, and passionate exhortation, it calls both individual Christians and the church collectively to take seriously the biblical laments. These essays need to be read carefully, because as they are read they will lead to heartfelt change, and Christians will learn afresh to weep with those who weep."

—Daniel J. Estes, Distinguished Professor of Old Testament
Cedarville University, Cedarville, Ohio

"Profound confusion, emotional distress, spiritual failures, and physical hardships are all too characteristic of our collective life together. Moreover, many are bewildered by the deep social crises experienced in our world. With biblical depth, theological insight, ethical concern, and pastoral care, *A Time for Sorrow* is a book that speaks to the human condition. It challenges us to recapture the important role of lament in the life of the church. May the church embody and practice what the gospel has preached!"

—**Patrick T. Smith, Associate Research Professor of Theological Ethics and Bioethics, Duke Divinity School**

"The church needs to learn how to lament. Here is an important book for pastors and lay leaders explaining the biblical, theological, and historical reasons why. As a pastor responsible for planning corporate worship, I was challenged and encouraged by this book to make the biblical practice of lament a regular part of our church's gatherings—not only for the care of God's people, but also for the sake of our mission to a hurting world. If you are a leader in Christ's church, *A Time for Sorrow* will help you understand the urgent need and biblical imperative to recover the lost practice of lament."

—**Nicholas Lauer, Co-Pastor Trinity Baptist Church, New Haven, Connecticut**

"The authors of this volume each present us with unique insights while echoing a common theme—that lament is natural, beneficial, and, most of all, good. It is the appropriate response to the human experience of trauma, modeled by Jesus and proclaimed in Scripture. Most importantly, *A Time for Sorrow* serves as a much-needed clarion call to recover and promote the practice of lament—whether alone or in community, whether as sufferer or empathizer—as a discipline integral to a healthy spiritual life."

—**R. Brian Siebeking, Assistant Professor of Religious Studies Gonzaga University, Spokane, Washington**

"I have read many references on lament in the Bible. *A Time for Sorrow* is by far one of the most helpful in promoting the practice of lament for the church today. It provides a good foundation for understanding lament, not only from the Old Testament but also from the New Testament. I find the treatment on the latter comprehensive and convincing. The book also provides a good theological discussion and practical advice on the practice of lament in the context of the church. I highly recommend this book!"

—**Federico G. Villanueva General Editor, Asia Bible Commentary Series Author of *The Uncertainty of a Hearing: A Study of the Sudden Change of Mood in the Psalms of Lament***

# A Time for Sorrow

*Recovering the Practice of Lament
in the Life of the Church*

Edited by
Scott Harrower & Sean M. McDonough

A Time for Sorrow: Recovering the Practice of Lament
in the Life of the Church

© 2019 by Hendrickson Publishers Marketing, LLC
P. O. Box 3473
Peabody, Massachusetts 01961–3473
www.hendrickson.com

ISBN 978-1-68307-206-5

All rights reserved. No part of this book may be reproduced or transmitted in any form or by any means, electronic or mechanical, including photocopying, recording, or by any information storage and retrieval system, without permission in writing from the publisher.

Scripture quotations marked CSB®, are taken from the Holman Christian Standard Bible®, Copyright © 1999, 2000, 2002, 2003, 2009, 2017 by Holman Bible Publishers. Used by permission. CSB® is a federally registered trademark of Holman Bible Publishers.

Scripture quotations marked (ESV) are taken from the Holy Bible, English Standard Version (ESV®), copyright © 2001 by Crossway, a publishing ministry of Good News Publishers. Used by permission. All rights reserved.

Scripture quotations marked (NIV) are taken from the Holy Bible, New International Version®, NIV®. Copyright © 1973, 1978, 1984, 2011 by Biblica, Inc.™ Used by permission of Zondervan. All rights reserved worldwide. www.zondervan.com. The "NIV" and "New International Version" are trademarks registered in the United States Patent and Trademark Office by Biblica, Inc.™

*Printed in the United States of America*

*First Printing — September 2019*

Cover image:
**Vincent van Gogh (1853–90)**
Congregation Leaving the Reformed Church in Nuenen
Nuenen, January – February 1884 and autumn 1885
oil on canvas, 41.3 x 32.1 cm
Van Gogh Museum, Amsterdam (Vincent van Gogh Foundation)
s3V1962
F25

**Library of Congress Cataloging-in-Publication**

Names: Harrower, Scott D., editor.
Title: A time for sorrow : recovering the practice of lament in the life of
    the church / edited by Scott Harrower and Sean McDonough.
Description: Peabody, MA : Hendrickson Publishers, 2019. | Includes
    bibliographical references.
Identifiers: LCCN 2019007459 | ISBN 9781683072065 (alk. paper)
Subjects: LCSH: Grief--Religious aspects--Christianity. |
    Bereavement--Religious aspects--Christianity. | Laments in the Bible.
Classification: LCC BV4905.3 .T488 2019 | DDC 248.8/6--dc23
LC record available at https://lccn.loc.gov/2019007459

# Contents

| | |
|---|---|
| Introduction: Why Lament Matters<br>*Sean M. McDonough and Scott Harrower* | 1 |
| 1. Lament as a Prayer of Faith<br>*Lindsay Wilson* | 5 |
| 2. Lament in the Book of Ezekiel: Its Purpose and Function<br>*Donna Petter* | 23 |
| 3. Lament among Evangelicals: Historical Reflections on Pastoral Practice<br>*Rhys S. Bezzant* | 37 |
| 4. Lament in the New Testament<br>*Sean M. McDonough* | 53 |
| 5. God the Trinity and Christian Care for Those Who Lament<br>*Scott Harrower* | 69 |
| 6. "There Is a Balm in Gilead": A Call to Lament Together<br>*Emmett G. Price III* | 89 |
| Notes | 101 |
| Bibliography | 119 |
| List of Contributors | 129 |

# Introduction

## WHY LAMENT MATTERS

Sean M. McDonough and Scott Harrower

People want to be happy. It is not surprising, then, that modern churches often seek to create a purely positive, upbeat worship environment. People come to be inspired and uplifted, and they want to leave feeling contented about God, the world, and themselves.

That is the plan, anyway. In reality, of course, the throngs of peppy parishioners still carry around disappointments, grievances, hidden sins, and all manner of physical and emotional troubles. Some of the causes of lament are obvious: the death of a loved one, a painful divorce, a terminal diagnosis. But people can often be ground down toward despair by the gradual wear and tear of everyday life. They feel trapped in a job they hate but cannot give up. Their children seem unable to get the hang of adult life and become a source of perpetual disappointment. They find themselves friendless in a soulless new city. If the gap between the relentless positivity of worship and the unyielding difficulty of life becomes too great, they may simply stop coming to church altogether, under the (often correct) assumption that the church really does not know how to deal with their problems.

The good news is that God offers a different way forward. In addition to the roads of thanksgiving and praise, the Bible acknowledges that God's people often need to walk the way of lament—a path on which life's ills can be openly shared with God in the confidence that he is big enough to handle them.

This volume is intended to assist the church in recapturing the biblical practice of lament. Drawing on the major theological disciplines—Old and New Testament studies, church history, and dogmatic and practical theology—we explore the benefits that flow from a faithful approach to God that brings before him all of our lives, not just the positive bits. We will see that the individual and corporate recognition of life's struggles is fully endorsed by Scripture and should be an integral part of church practice.

The first essay, "Lament as a Prayer of Faith" by Old Testament professor Lindsay Wilson, serves as an overview of the theme of lament in Scripture, with special emphasis on the need to recapture lament in the contemporary church. Professor Wilson's expertise in Job and the Psalms serves him well as he leads us through the biblical witness on lament.

Another Old Testament scholar, Donna Petter, devotes her attention to the theme of lament in the book of Ezekiel. She delves into the specifics of Ezekiel's historical situation and then draws out a critical pastoral point: Lament should not only address situations of personal distress, but it should also give voice to sorrow over sin. Even when the consequences of our sinful choices are unavoidable, a repentant heart is the first step in the restoration God desires for his people.

Rhys Bezzant next offers an historical perspective in his piece "Lament among Evangelicals: Historical Reflections on Pastoral Practice." Bezzant—a scholar of church history, theology, and Christian worship—demonstrates that the evangelical church's ability to properly lament has been hamstrung by a persistent need to pursue social and political power rather than to embrace gospel weakness. As he puts it, "There is . . . in our story an allergic reaction at almost every point to feelings of powerlessness."

Sean McDonough explores "Lament in the New Testament." He begins by noting that Old Testament lament texts were very much in play in the early church. He then shows how the call to "rejoice in the Lord" is balanced by Jesus and the apostles with the acknowledgment of human frailty and the ongoing need to bring our sorrows before the Lord.

Scott Harrower combines biblical exposition with theological reflection in his essay "God the Trinity and Christian Care for Those Who Lament." He focuses on the question of divine empathy and action for those recovering from trauma, and the ways in which God's triune nature serves as a balm to those who have undergone life-shattering experiences. He finds Paul's second letter to the Corinthians to be of particular relevance to victims of trauma.

Finally, Emmett Price—professor of worship, church, and culture and founding executive director of the Institute for the Study of the Black Christian Experience at Gordon-Conwell Theological Seminary—explores the role of lament in congregational life in "'There Is a Balm in Gilead:' A Call to Lament Together." Drawing upon the often unrecognized anguish of the African-American community and other beleaguered peoples, he challenges the church at large to "weep with those who weep" and embrace the way of lament as the path toward a more just and compassionate body of Christ.

We pray that these essays will be an encouragement to all who care about the progress of God's kingdom, and who know that its path is often paved with lament—and who also know that while "weeping may stay for the night . . . rejoicing comes in the morning" (Ps. 30:5).

# 1

# LAMENT AS A PRAYER OF FAITH

Lindsay Wilson

## Introduction: Lament Has Been Neglected in the Christian Church

A popularly held view in Christian circles is "that to express lament is necessarily to take up a stance of doubt and unbelief; that verbalizing words of grief to God represents a lack of spiritual maturity rather than being an acceptable, even mandated, response to life in a broken world."[1] Thus we often counsel someone to suffer without complaining. Yet, have you ever wondered if there is room for something more than submissive trust when confronted with a great loss? Do we cease to be human when we become a Christian, or are we more human than ever?[2]

A Filipino friend of mine, Rico Villanueva, has written a small insightful book, *It's OK to Be Not OK: The Message of the Lament Psalms*. He notes the following in today's churches:

There's no room for:

- Negative emotions like despair/sadness/loneliness; fear; anger

- Negative actions like struggling; mourning/weeping/crying; questioning God

- Negative situations like failure; accidents; calamities

Generally today, it's not OK to be down; it's not OK to be sad; it's not OK to cry; it's not OK to be afraid; it's not OK to struggle; it's not OK to be angry; it's not OK to question God; it's not OK to fail.[3]

The net result is that the laments have "all but disappeared from Christian prayer."[4] It appears that the lament has been both deliberately ignored and subtly replaced. The negativity of lament seems to be on a different wavelength to our world, which is so strongly committed to the need to be positive and affirming. Hence, P. H. Kelley notes that the lament "has been repudiated by purveyors of positive thinking."[5] In many Christian circles, we are urged to "claim the victory," rather than complain or lament.

In September 2012, Todd Billings, a Reformed systematic theologian at Western Theological Seminary, was diagnosed with incurable blood cancer at the age of thirty-nine. In *Rejoicing in Lament*, he shares,

> My response was not simple. At times I would cry out in grief to God; along with this, I would lament in protest to God for the sake of my young children. At times I responded in gratitude for—and awe of— all of the gifts that God had already given, even if my life were not to be extended much longer.[6]

Since his diagnosis, he describes how he experienced the neglect of laments in churches to be "a stinging loss." "Cherry-picking only the praises from the Psalms tends to shape a church culture in which only positive emotions can be expressed before God in faith."[7]

Over the past forty years, there have begun to be a number of champions of prayers of lament, urging us to rediscover the lament and its contribution to individual and corporate prayer.[8] Walter Brueggemann comments that "the lament psalms offer important resources for Christian faith and ministry even though they have been largely purged from the life of the church and its liturgical use."[9] While this rediscovery of lament emerged mainly from that curious breed of creatures, "biblical scholars" or "Christian academics," I am not persuaded that the majority of everyday Christians or even Christian ministers are convinced about the value of lament.

Perhaps it is time to take a fresh look at the lament as a valuable resource for Christian prayer, and this is now where I want to turn.

# What Is Lament?

## It Is Widespread in the Old Testament

You would never guess it from Christian hymns or songs based on the Psalms, but laments make up about 40 percent of the Psalms. Lament is at the core of the book of Job, as he struggles to hold on to his faith, and prophets such as Jeremiah and Habakkuk express their anguish in words of lament.[10] And, as its name suggests, the entire book of Lamentations is lament.

## It Is One Form of Petitionary Prayer

What, then, makes up the lament? While there is no rigid form for them, Claus Westermann points out that "the lament . . . has its fixed, regularly recurring parts."[11] The basic skeletal structure of individual and community laments typically includes an invocation, the lament or complaint itself, a review of God's past help (or expression of confidence), petition, and a vow to praise (or actual praise).

Several important aspects of the lament are crucial. First, the focus of the lament is not just the complaint, for it is fundamentally a plea or petition for help. Westermann rightly observes that "petition, or at any rate something like petition, intrinsically belongs to the lament."[12] The fact that the writers continue after the complaint is uttered shows that the mere pouring out of a complaint is not the goal. A lament is not just a venting of feelings, nor is it intended to stop with the voicing of the complaint. Those lamenting seek a resolution of their distress, since the lament is an appeal for help.[13] It is not simply a complaint about God; it is addressed to God. A lament is asking for change from the God who is able to bring about change.

Second, the lament is not static, but is heading toward a goal. This is essentially moving through one's present trouble in order to turn in praise to God. "Anger is not the final word. Almost without exception, the lament concludes on a note of confidence and hope, trust and joy."[14] The only individual lament psalm not to end with praise or a vow to praise is Psalm 88, though even here the linked psalm titles of Psalms 87 through 89 suggest that Psalm 88 is to be read alongside, and lead into, the praise in Psalm 89.[15] It is the present circumstances of the lamenter that are found to be overwhelming; yet as they are expressed, the worshipper is able to clarify his settled convictions and turn expectantly to God. Thus the complaint is expressed in order to move on in a relationship with God.

Lament is designed to bring about change, and so Job, David, and the prophets lament in order to change or restore their relationship with God.

### *It Is Addressed to God and Moves toward Him*

A striking feature of the lament is that, even in the darkest times of feeling forsaken by God, the sufferers still lament and complain to God. Though their complaints include blame and rebuke, the underlying dynamic is to restore their relationship with God. These are expressions of a faith not shaken by God's seeming silence. Thus the movement within the lament is of crucial significance—the move from questioning to a restored relationship. Yet a lament does not skip too quickly to hope and praise. It lingers on the present distress and allows it to be expressed and faced. Of course, the lament does not stop at complaining, for the deeper goal is to reestablish a renewed relationship with God

Laments contain bold questions and even accusations leveled against God, but God is still the one to whom the lamenter turns. They still firmly believe that God is the one in charge. So, for example, Job's core complaints are addressed throughout to God, which marks them off from the speeches of his friends. Thus Francis Andersen comments that "his friends talk about God. Job talks to God."[16]

### *It Includes Complaint, Strong Emotion, Protest, and Even Accusation*

While some in our Western societies view crying as a sign of weakness, we are better served to follow Gandalf, who in Tolkien's *Lord of the Rings* observes, "I will not say: do not weep; for not all tears are an evil."[17] Tears are often a natural human response to loss and a healing expression of grief. Strong, "negative" emotions may be frowned upon in the church, but they are part of the fabric of biblical laments.

Psalm 13 is often given as a parade example of an individual lament and may help us to ground our observations. In verses 1–2, the psalmist pours out the depths of his despair in complaint to God. His questions are complaints that express how he sees his desperate situation, and they lay the blame at God's feet. He describes his plight as:

- Being forgotten by God (forever, utterly, continually).

- Being out of relationship with God. God has hidden his face from the writer. The image is of a broken relationship that is no longer face-to-face.

- Having pain and hurt within ("sorrow in my heart").

- Grief, sorrow, and loss with no end in sight.

- All of these are made worse because the enemy of God and the writer seem to be in the right because of God's apparent absence.

Here is the frustration: God appears to be absent, silent, and seemingly unconcerned (v. 1), yet pain and grief are present. Furthermore, the presence of pain and grief and God's seeming absence are exacerbated by the haunting presence of the enemies.

In verses 3–4, the writer turns to God and protests about how God is managing the world, and there is an implied rebuke directed to God.

- Look! Answer me—this is not a cool, dispassionate request to "consider" the situation. Indignation, anger, and the feeling of being unfairly treated are all bubbling up.

- Yet he knows that if anything is to be done about his situation, only God is able to do it—and so he calls out to the one he addresses as "Lord my God." It is his big view of God that causes him problems. If he did not believe that God was in absolute control, he could at least understand why he was suffering. But he will not try to trim down his understanding of God even if that would make it easier.

- He voices a desperate petition—it's now or never, God! "Look on me and answer." Come to my aid! Deliver me!

- Again, the presence of enemies exacerbates his situation. The enemy here may be death personified, or it may have been the actual enemies of the writer, but their role is clear. This time, it is filled out by reference to the content of their taunting—"I have overcome him" (v. 4)—and their callous reaction of rejoicing at the writer's pain and loss.

- Until now, it has been a picture of deep despair—a person out of relationship with God and his fellow humans, disoriented in an alien world. Perhaps the only flicker of hope—a faint one, almost snuffed out—is that the writer is at least still turning to God in prayer, even though there seems to be no answer. He continues to cling on to his God, although his God seems absent or, even worse, against him. Up to this point in the psalm, the writer persists, in the face of grief and pain and in wrestling with God in a struggle for authentic faith.

Interestingly, this psalm does not end with the writer stuck in his despair. Between verses 4 and 5, something has happened. Perhaps his circumstances have now changed, or there is a change within him. It is commonly suggested that a prophetic oracle of salvation, or cultic word of assurance, was uttered here.[18] Yet the precise identity of what happened is unexplained and apparently not where our focus should be. The very fact that no details are given enables this psalm to have a wider use in a variety of situations. What is crucial is that something has brought him to see that his God does care and is for him. Thus he rejoices in a deliverance that either has already happened or has been promised (v. 5). He has experienced God's committed, unfailing, steadfast love. The Hebrew word order in the original makes it even clearer that the focus is on God's covenant love. He has no doubt that God is faithful, and he now asserts the very point he questioned. What was at stake in the first part of this psalm was that the writer did not feel cared for by God, that he was cut off from God's love. Thus he now responds in singing praise to God based on God's character (his "unfailing love") and his actions ("salvation," "deliverance," CSB).

Of course, the writer records all this after the event, after God has delivered him. Yet, unlike many of the hymns of praise in the Psalms, he does not simply record God's actions and his glad response. He still records the darkness, the disorientation, the despair of that seemingly endless time before he was delivered. That is the beauty of the lament. It ends with a reminder of God's faithfulness and his deliverance, but it does not seek to deny just how hard those hard times were. It deals fairly with both the harshness of God seeming not to care and the joy of finally coming to see his faithfulness. The movement within the lament is therefore of crucial significance—the move from questioning to praise gives full weight to both.[19] God's verdict on the laments is seen even more clearly in the book of Job, where God twice commends what Job has said to him or about him (Job 42:7–8).

## *It Can Include Repentance but Need Not Do So*

One of the features of the lament psalms is that they do not normally include the confession of sin. Of course, the book of Psalms includes repentance and confession of sin, which is what we see in penitential psalms such as Psalm 51.[20] But confession is not a frequent feature of laments. Laments focus primarily on the pain of loss itself, often at the hands of enemies of different kinds. There is little focus on what the individual or even the community has contributed to the loss (for example, through sin).

In biblical scholarship, lament has been overshadowed by an emphasis on the need for repentance from sin. Indeed, Westermann has proposed that "the confession of sin has become the Christianized form of the lament."[21] The suffering presupposed in a lament is seen to pale into insignificance in comparison to the drastic consequences of sin and guilt.

Yet, does this need to be an either/or situation? Does a high view of sin necessarily lead to minimizing the reality of suffering and despair? Is there not room for both? To lament one's circumstances is not necessarily to deny one's sinfulness, simply to assert that the present difficulties are not the outworking of judgment on sin. In the book of Job, it is the friends who decree that his suffering is due to sin and that the way to restoration is confession. As readers, we see that their analysis does not square with the prologue (chapters 1–2). Job's response is not to confess any sin but to lament his situation, a stance endorsed by God himself at the conclusion of the book (Job 42:7–8).[22]

In the end, our deepest need is not to understand why our suffering or loss has occurred, but to know if God cares and can be trusted. So the key issue is how we will respond to God in the midst of suffering. Jerry Sittser, a Christian professor in the United States, watched his mother, his wife of twenty years, and his four-year-old daughter die after a speeding car jumped its lane and crashed head on into his minivan. Three generations, all gone in an instant. In the weeks and months after the tragedy, Sittser said he felt he was being punished by simply being alive and thought death would bring a welcome relief. But he came out the other side of darkness, and in *A Grace Disguised*, he wrote these words: "The experience of loss does not need to be the defining moment of our lives. Instead, the defining moment can be *our response* to the loss."[23] John Goldingay reminds us that the Old Testament "does not seek to explain suffering but to help people live with it. . . . The question it raises is whether we can hold onto God and onto hope."[24] At their heart, that is what the laments are trying to do.

Yet, there is some room in lament for repentance as well. Especially in the community laments, we find acknowledgement of sin and confession. This is most clearly seen in the book of Lamentations—a whole book of laments—as Israel sought to come to terms with the destruction of Jerusalem and the exile of God's chosen people. They graphically pour out their pain and loss in lament:

How deserted lies the city, once so full of people! How like a widow is she, who once was great among the nations! . . . Bitterly she weeps at night, tears are upon her cheeks. . . . [T]here is none to comfort her. All her friends have betrayed her; they have become her enemies. (Lam. 1:1–2)

But the exile they were now experiencing came about as a result of their disobedience to God over many years and their sinful neglect of his word and promises. They still lament their loss and pour out their grief, but they also admit their sin:

My sins have been bound into a yoke. (Lam. 1:14)

The Lord is in the right, yet I rebelled against his command. (Lam. 1:18)

Deal with them as you have dealt with me because of all my sins. (Lam. 1:22)

Lament and confession are not mutually exclusive, but we need to be careful not to press people into confessing sin when they actually need to lament their loss. This is what Job's friends failed to understand, and God said of them, "You have not spoken of me what is right" (Job 42:7–8).

## What Is the Value of Lament?

### It Expresses Raw Honesty before God

The book of Job affirms that the honest pouring out to God of our deepest hurts, our raw emotions, even our strongest accusations, is an appropriate way to channel our pain. It is always appropriate to be honest before the God of the theophany who knows and sustains all things. God will never be "blown away" by the strength of our language. Daniel Simundson suggests that "the lament gives the sufferer words to use, a way of bringing into the open what is difficult to express, so that it may be acknowledged and worked through in some meaningful process."[25]

No one would suggest that complaint or lament is at the core of Israelite faith. Yet, the Old Testament laments are presented as a legitimate part of faith when people undergo unspeakable loss and suffering and experience God as silent or absent. Complaint can then be a proper expression of anguish and a desire to have their relationship with God restored.[26] In such situations, these biblical laments reflect a fundamental trust in God despite the lamenter's circumstances. Just as belief and doubt can mark the life of a believer, so too can praise and lament. Faith includes responding not only to life's delights but also to its difficulties. Since God has made us as humans with raw emotions, there must be some opportunity to process them in a way that will enable us to keep on believing in a good and powerful God.

It is of course Job's strident, even accusing, words of protest addressed to God in the dialogue that seem to sit most awkwardly with his earlier piety. In 6:4, he complains:

> The arrows of the Almighty are in me,
>   my spirit drinks in their poison;
>   God's terrors are marshalled against me.

This does not sound like a typical comment made at morning tea after church, for he is suggesting that God is firing (metaphorical) poisoned arrows at him and terrifying him. At this point, some ministers I know would offer him a cup of tea in the hope that this would settle him down.

Job accuses God of making him his target (7:20) and multiplying his wounds without cause (9:17). He complains that God is oppressing and despising him (10:3), hiding his face from Job and counting him as an enemy (13:24). Indeed, he pictures God as having mounted a full-scale attack on him (16:7–16).

Can true faith include such statements, accusations, and protests, or has Job overstepped the boundaries of genuine godliness? What is often missed about Job's bold words is that he is assuming that God is in absolute control of what happens in his world. What

Job is experiencing could happen only because God either permitted or caused it. This big view of God is behind his accusatory words. It may not be "church-speak," but it is certainly "God-speak." The world is not reduced to a secular closed circle of cause and effect from which God is excluded. If it happens in God's world, Job sees God as the one to turn to in the midst of life's struggle. He honestly and openly describes what he understands from his faith position.

But how does God evaluate his words at the end of the book (42:7–8)? He rebukes Eliphaz: "I am angry with you and your two friends, because you have not spoken the truth about me, as my servant Job has." This is perhaps not what many expect to hear, but it is what we find in Scripture. So, as Roland Murphy expresses it, "One of the significant gifts of the book [of Job] is honest language in conversing with God."[27]

## *Lamenters Talk to God Rather Than Taking a Time-Out*

Kathleen Farmer notes that those who lament "do not wait passively for God to notice their pain and come to their aid. Rather, they cry out as an act of faith in the steadfast love of the one they confidently trust will not reject them for what they feel or say."[28] In Old Testament studies, Brueggemann has been particularly attuned to the value of lament in a life of faith. He writes that "the faith expressed in the lament is nervy, that honest facing of distress can only be done effectively in dialogue with God who acts in transforming ways."[29] It is easier in the midst of trials to give up rather than to hang on.

Think about what you might have done if you were in Job's sandals. He does not take time out from his relationship with God. Job does call on God to leave him alone (7:16; 10:20; 14:6), but this is only part of the picture. He still asks God to "remember" him and what he is like (7:7; 10:9; 14:13), and it is Job who keeps on initiating conversation with God as he characteristically turns in his speeches from talking to his friends (6:1–30; 12:1–13:19) to addressing God (7:1–21; 13:20–14:22). His deepest longing is not for God's absence but for his restored presence (14:15). And so he keeps on talking to God, even as he complains to him.

In 14:15a, Job's overarching goal is well expressed: "You will call, and I will answer you." In other words, lamenting for Job is the only way of clinging on to a God who seems silent or absent. Rather than an embarrassment to faith, the laments of the Old Testament are a challenge to genuine faith in the midst of trouble—a faith that knows that, even when God seems silent, help can come from no one else except God. This is not a failure of faith but a part of a genuine faith that has the courage to doubt, to complain, to protest—knowing that God and God alone can meet him in his utter darkness. So, "even words of doubt expressed to God become statements of faith because they are addressed to the right person."[30] This is not a laid-back, easy-going faith we find here, but a desperate struggle of faith, for faith—trying to make sense of the world around him in the light of what he knows about God.

### *Lamenters Believe That God Is Big Enough to Take Their Pain*

The laments are a legitimate part of a robust adult faith that knows God will not be shattered or provoked by strong words of protest. God does not, unlike many of us, avoid conflict, for he knows that the honest expression of our current situation is essential for our transformation. To ask where God is in the midst of one's sufferings is based on faith that God could do something about the circumstances if he chose. Desmond Tutu, as he reflected on the struggle in South Africa, has pointed out that the perplexity behind laments comes from a belief that God is good, loving, and powerful. This big view of God creates the problem when God does not seem to act in response to those calling out to him.[31]

What are some of the identifying characteristics of Job's protesting faith? He continues to insist that the solution must be found with God and therefore keeps on talking to him. In the face of unimaginable difficulty, he continues to direct his gaze and his words to God. He does not turn away when it becomes too hard. To pursue

God into uncharted territory takes greater faith than the approach of his friends, who attempt to tidy up their messy world with a series of glib propositions about what must be true. Choon-Leong Seow rightly observes: "To Job . . . people who are afraid of confronting the tough, faith-shattering questions are not fearers of God. Rather, they are simply fearers, theological cowards, for they fear the truth."[32] It is Job, not the friends, who demonstrate a robust faith.

Faith encompasses trusting God in the midst of distress, not simply thinking positively once the adverse circumstances have passed. It is possible to show faith even when God does not appear to answer our cries for help or apparently fails to act on our behalf. It is not dependent on change (in us or our circumstances) already having taken place. Faith looks to God as the one who is able to help, and who is strong enough not to be shaken by an outpouring of our pain. It is not expressed in glib words but emerges from a deep commitment to cling on to the God we have known, no matter what. Sadly, faith like this today is more likely to be found among the persecuted church in the majority world than in the lives of comfortable Christians in the West.

## *Lament Is an Alternative to "False Repentance"*

In the midst of overwhelming hardship, what alternatives are there? Indeed, what do we do in our struggles? I suspect that we often react to God in one of two ways. We either pretend that all is rosy or we take "time out" and avoid having to face God. The first—living a life of pretense—is dishonest. If we feel angry, overwhelmed, or confused and we pretend as we pray that all is well, we put up a front that is trying to push God away. Our faith and our God become less and less real. God prefers to relate to us as we are, rather than as we pretend to be. Job, for example, resisted the temptation to go through the motions of repenting so that God would have to ease his suffering and restore his blessings—which was the response suggested by his friends. Throughout the dialogue of this book, Job is constantly accused of being a person who has abandoned his former faith in God (Job 1:1, 8; 2:3). Eliphaz, Bildad, and Zophar all accuse Job of some form of sin that warrants his present suffering (e.g., Job 4:17; 8:3–6; 11:4–6). In addition, the human verdict of Elihu is that Job's words are those of "unfaith" (e.g., Job 34:7–9). Walter Brueggemann, referring to the lament psalms, notes:

> The use of these "psalms of darkness" may be judged by the world to be acts of unfaith and failure, but for the trusting community, their use is an act of bold faith, albeit a transformed faith. It is an act of bold faith on the one hand, because it insists that the world must be experienced as it really is and not in some pretended way. On the other hand, it is bold because it insists that all such experiences of disorder are a proper subject for discourse with God. There is nothing out of bounds, nothing precluded or inappropriate. Everything properly belongs in this conversation of the heart.[33]

Taking time out from our relationship with God is no better—no longer praying or reading God's word, avoiding our Christian friends. We waste days, weeks, months, living as if we're on our own—closing ourselves off from God and others. Tragically, some give up their faith entirely: they no longer have anything to do with God and his people, and they become bitter and twisted.

The laments offer a different response to these two options. They are expressions of a faith that refuse to surrender despite difficult circumstances, a faith that knows that its only solution is with God, even when God himself seems to neither hear nor care. Those who utter these laments pour out to God their honest reaction to whatever has befallen them. They do not cease speaking to God, nor do they pretend and play games with him. They pour out their hearts, hoping against hope that God will intervene and answer their longings. While it is sometimes inappropriate to share our deepest feelings with one another, it always appropriate to bring them to God. Of course, that is not all there is to faith, nor is it an end in itself; but it is so often a helpful and legitimate stage in working toward the goal of trusting God in the midst of troubles. We can be too quick in moving to an easy, half-baked trust.

We do need to move on from lamenting to see God's faithfulness afresh, but we will not do so if we bottle up our hurts and our anger, or pretend they do not exist. We need to lay out our inner sufferings before the one who can change both us and our circumstances, helping us through our trials to a deeper, growing trust in our God.

## Lament Is Not Overridden by the Death and Resurrection of Jesus

### Lament Is Not Sub-Christian

Geoff Harper cites some common objections to laments:

> Ought not mature Christian spirituality to be permeated with the victory that is ours in Christ? . . . Did the psalmists not learn the secret of being content in all circumstances? Did they not know that God is sovereign, that he works all things for the good of those who love him?"[34]

Indeed, many Christians have been quick to censor and discard the laments, based on an implicit understanding of them as embarrassing, perhaps even sub-Christian. Billings, however, argues that "lament is part of the Christian life until the final kingdom comes.[35]

The words of God must control our reading of laments. In the book of Job, for example, God actually reflects on whether Job was right to speak as he did. God's verdict is that not only was Job blameless and upright at the beginning (1:8; 2:3), but also that what Job said about God during the debate was right (42:7–8). In the dialogue, Job speaks to his friends about God in laments. God must therefore be endorsing at least the general thrust of Job's laments and complaints. One writer says, "'Theodicy' is what relatively healthy people think about in the face of suffering. *Lament* is what sufferers must do—it is the voice of theodicy in life."[36]

### Lament in the New Testament

David Burge asks the reasonable question: "If lament is an acceptable activity for Christians, why is it not endorsed more prominently in the New Testament?" Then he provides his own answer: "The New Testament writings affirm the validity of lament by observing its normative presence in the lives and teachings of Jesus and his three most prominent apostles—Peter, Paul, and in a cursory way, John."[37] In particular, he points out that "Christ's death and resurrection has not done away with lament."[38] How can such an approach be justified?

Some look at the lament tone of the Beatitudes, where God pronounces as "blessed" those who mourn (Matt 5:4).[39] Others point to Jesus' words on the cross. In his genuine humanness, with the awfulness of the sin of the world separating him from the Father, he turns to Psalm 22 and utters those now-familiar words, "My God, my God, why have you forsaken me?" (Mark 15:34). Indeed, Hebrews 5:7 tells us that "Jesus offered up prayers and petitions with fervent cries and tears to the one who could save him from death, and he was heard because of his reverent submission."

In the midst of his suffering as an apostle, Paul expresses his deep pain when he speaks of pleading with God to remove his unidentified thorn of flesh:

> So to keep me from becoming conceited because of the surpassing greatness of the revelations, a thorn was given me in the flesh, a messenger of Satan to harass me, to keep me from becoming conceited. Three times I pleaded with the Lord about this, that it should leave me. (2 Cor. 12:7–8)

Burge also reminds us that "the Paul who says 'be joyful always' can also say in Rom 9:1–3 'I have great sorrow and unceasing anguish. . . . The historical Paul, the real Paul, was no stranger to suffering, weakness, and lament."[40]

So, too, the early church, undergoing persecution, cries out to God in lament: How long? In Revelation 6:9–11 we read,

> When he opened the fifth seal, I saw under the altar the souls of those who had been slain for the word of God and for the witness they had borne. They cried out with a loud voice, "O Sovereign Lord, holy and true, how long before you will judge and avenge our blood on those

who dwell on the earth?" Then they were each given a white robe and told to rest a little longer, until the number of their fellow servants and their brothers should be complete, who were to be killed as they themselves had been.[41]

In recent scholarship, Rebekah Eklund in *Jesus Wept* explores laments in the New Testament.[42] Articles have also emerged from Keith Campbell on lament in James, from Don West on the shape and function of New Testament lament, and from David Burge on the place of lament in the New Testament.[43]

## Lament Is Still Pastorally Useful in the Church and the World Today

In our own times, we need to relearn how to lament as we look at our world: when we see that selfishness and pride have become a national way of life; when we see the wicked prosper; when Christians are persecuted; when, in our churches, spiritual coldness and division are rampant; when people around us harden their hearts, as they ridicule the gospel and mock the name of Christ. With all of this we, too, need to cry out and lament. There is much in this world that seems so wrong and should drive us to God with honest questions. And so, those who lament do not stop speaking to God. They pour out their hearts, hoping against hope that God will hear and answer. Lamenting to God is perhaps better than a path of silent submission, for that would not provide room for the expression of the loss or the petition for a restored relationship. Malcolm Gill comments, "As people read the laments there is often the underlying thought, 'That is exactly how I feel, but I could never say that to God.'"[44] Lamentation makes connections with many in today's world.

Lamentation is also a kind of raw honesty with God, and its expression is often a helpful and legitimate stage in working toward the goal of trusting God in the midst of troubles. There is great value in laying out our inner sufferings before the one who can change both us and our circumstances, helping us through to a deeper, growing faith in our God.

What should we lament over? Consider random shootings in churches around the world; senseless acts of violence; lands devastated by a typhoon or tsunami; young children and infants starving to death or dying of cancer; persecuted Christians in North Korea, Sudan, the Middle East; the hardness of hearts of many to the gospel in the Western world.[45] Some of these events, I don't understand and most I can't change. I don't run short of situations in which I can lament. I simply run out of time to pray for them all.[46]

# Conclusion

As David J. Cohen observes, "God is attentive to our laments in the same way that God is attentive to our praises."[47] Followers of God need a language that will express their deepest feelings to God, in times of joy and in times of great suffering and anguish.[48] The Bible provides both in songs of praise and thanks—and in laments. Real life is not always easy, and laments provide resources to help us live out real lives before God.

Nancy Duff expresses it well when she says,

> Psalms of lament allow us to speak from the darkest regions of the heart, where our despair threatens to overwhelm us. In so speaking we do not exhibit a lack of faith, but stand in a biblical tradition that recognizes that no part of life, including the most hideous and painful parts, is to be withheld from God.[49]

This is ultimately a stance of faith—genuine, honest, persevering faith. And so, I do lament about the loss of lament among evangelical Christians today.

# 2

# LAMENT IN THE BOOK OF EZEKIEL: ITS PURPOSE AND FUNCTION

Donna Petter

## Introduction

Ezekiel may not be the book that first comes to mind relative to the topic of lamentation. In fact, most people only think of Ezekiel when it comes to the mysterious temple envisioned in chapters 40–48—a subject that has occupied not a little space in scholarly circles and in the church relative to its fulfillment. Was it Ezra's temple (Ezra 6:13–18)? A rebuilt millennial temple? A picture of God's presence through the Holy Spirit in the church? A temple related to the new heavens and earth? Others are mesmerized with Ezekiel's strange opening vision of the living creatures (Ezek. 1:4–21), and some labor to know the identity of Gog and Magog (Ezek. 38–39). Still others love to sing about "dem dry bones, dem dry bones" to hear the Word of the Lord (Ezek. 37:1–10)!

In this chapter, we are going to put those valid interpretive questions aside to consider the book of Ezekiel and the theme of lamentation. Other than the bizarre incident of eating a scroll containing lamentation, mourning, and woe (Ezek. 3:2–3), a careful reading of the book reveals that lamentation is a dominant theme—something not merely confined to the scroll incident. I will attempt to demonstrate that by considering the main idea of the book, by looking at the theme of death, and through the consideration of Ezekiel's portrayal in the book (other than as a prophet), the presence of lamentation prevails in a surprising way with a critical purpose throughout this unique prophetic book. We will see from a pastoral perspective that Ezekiel has much to offer the church in its struggle to lament.

## The Presence of Lamentation in the Book of Ezekiel

### *The Main Idea of Ezekiel*

The book of Ezekiel shows repeated portraits of death and destruction for Israel. The nation and individuals must die. The city must fall. Sin plus judgment equates to death. This "death" is triggered by Israel's unrelenting sin of idolatry, which leads to Yahweh's unrelenting anger, both of which are vividly and tragically displayed in the vision of divine abandonment (Ezek. 8–11). In this vision, Ezekiel witnesses the slow and reluctant departure of Yahweh from the temple and city. Ultimately, death brings lamentation, mourning, and woe.

The book of Ezekiel also shows a stunning portrait of life and restoration for Israel. The nation and individuals will live. The city will be restored. This life is triggered by God's unrelenting loyalty to wayward people—something displayed in the vision of the rebuilt temple (Ezek. 40–48). In it, Ezekiel witnesses the return of Yahweh to his temple (43:1–5). It is a dramatic reversal of divine abandonment depicted in the earlier vision (Ezek. 8–11). The return is part of the larger work of restoration orchestrated supernaturally by God and is no less than a resurrection of sorts (Ezek. 36–48; esp. 37:1–14). Simply put, Ezekiel speaks of death (due to divine abandonment) but also the hope for life (due to the return of the divine presence). Out of death comes life.

Although the *removal and return* of a deity with respect to an earthly shrine is amply documented in the literature of the ancient world,[1] the twin theme of removal and return finds a home particularly in Mesopotamian city lament literature because this genre details and develops a city's fall and eventual rise again at great length.² Within this body of Mesopotamian lament literature, scholars recognize various overlapping literary features for mourning the death of a city. Following the work of F. W. Dobbs-Allsopp, these features include subject and mood, poetic devices, divine abandonment, assignment of responsibility, divine agents of destruction, destruction, a weeping goddess, lamentation, restoration of the city, and return of gods.³

A close reading of Ezekiel reveals that the book contains not only Yahweh's abandonment of (Ezek. 8–11) and return to a temple (Ezek. 43:1–5), but also the full repertoire of generic features found in the Mesopotamian city laments. Reflexes of city lament features appear throughout the book. The imprint of this city lament genre for the entire collection of his prophecies dated over a period of years is illustrated in how the mourning theme unfolds in the book.⁴ These features tie the book together from a literary perspective and might be seen as a logical and helpful literary means to illumine Ezekiel's main point: that Israel's sin of idolatry has led to the fall of Jerusalem.⁵ Indeed, the sad but anticipated announcement by the fugitive, "The city has fallen," reflects the emphasis on the city like no other prophet (Ezek. 33:21). As a result, the main subject matter in Ezekiel is the death and destruction of Jerusalem, its inhabitants, and Yahweh's temple. A prevailing mood of gloom looms large. Indeed, the scroll Ezekiel ate promised lamentation, mourning, and woe (2:9–3:2), and the book delivers on that promise.

## *The Theme of Death in the Book*

With very few exceptions, all of Ezekiel's prophetic words and dramatic signs (in chapters 4–24) illumine the death and destruction of the nation and associated contamination because of death. Indeed, death and destruction represent the natural consequences for rebels according to Deuteronomic Law (Deut. 28:15–68).

Shockingly, Ezekiel's audience earned themselves a less than attractive reputation (Ezek. 2:3–3:9). His service would be among people designated as rebels and idolaters, those who have rejected God's statutes and thus stand guilty before the Lord. In fact, eight chapters (Ezek. 16–23) deal extensively with the issue of Israel's past and present guilt through a variety of literary means. On the one hand, Israel's past is narrated through the metaphor of the unfaithful wife in which Jerusalem is portrayed as one who gives her affections to numerous others (Ezek. 16). On the other hand, through the metaphor of the unfaithful sisters, Jerusalem is portrayed as a woman desirous of love yet unsatisfied with what Yahweh has to offer (Ezek. 23).

Their rebellion and guilt has brought death and death-like consequences. Ezekiel describes human slaughter in Jerusalem and makes it clear that Yahweh is not a respecter of persons. Many victims will fall due to a merciless annihilation (9:6), which will produce massive amounts of corpses filling the land. Descriptions of destruction of the people and of the entire fabric of Israelite social, religious, and political customs fill the pages of Ezekiel.

In addition, death imagery surfaces throughout the book. Due to an experience with the supernatural, Ezekiel falls to his feet "as though dead" (1:28), and only with the Spirit's infusion does he stand on his feet and, in a manner of speaking, "return to life" (2:2). Ezekiel's watchman role concerns a warning pertaining to the death of a wicked person (3:18–19). In the tragic vision of God's glory leaving the temple, the man clothed in linen brings death to those without the mark, and Pelatiah dies right on the scene (11:13). Chapter 18 highlights death as the end for the one who sins, yet God clearly doesn't delight in the death of the wicked or anybody (18:23, 32)! Ezekiel experiences the death of his own wife as a painful visual aid for what lies ahead for the temple, the apple of the nation's eye (Ezek. 24:14). Both Tyre and its king die and are mourned (28:1). Egypt's demise, death, and burial are stunningly portrayed in poetic fashion, ending in a lament for both the nation and its pharaoh (32:17). And lastly, we read of the death and burial of Gog, which brings an end to all uncleanness (chs. 38–39).

Although the above represent key texts that speak of death, the vision of the valley of dry bones visualizes the extent of the problem (37:1–14). Ezekiel sees a field full of long-dead corpses on the valley's floor. It indicates that the people are as good as dead.

This vision mirrors their sentiment, "Our bones are dried up and our hope is gone; we are cut off" (37:11; 33:10). The question that God poses to Ezekiel—"Can these bones live?"—says it all. In other words, can life come out of death? Thus death and death imagery dominate in the book.

One expects that, as a natural result of death and death-like circumstances and the hopelessness felt and articulated by the people, lamentation would flow and find a natural expression. One expects that grief and sorrow would attend the exiles as a result. However, hardened, rebellious, and stubborn people with stiff foreheads (Ezek. 3:4–9) are unable to feel, much less grieve. Hardened people such as the exiles in Babylon were unable to grasp the gravity and theological realities of their circumstances. Hardened people cannot mourn.

Furthermore, they were incapable of mourning because they believed God would rescue them; indeed, they thought he was obliged to rescue them. After all, they were his people, Jerusalem was his holy dwelling, and the land was theirs due to divine promise. They failed to recognize that their present suffering was self-imposed—not because God had faltered, but because they faltered. They thought that God would save and shield them even from the consequences of their own rebellion. Death and destruction of this religious community as Ezekiel predicted did not fit their theological grid. Theologically blinded people cannot mourn.

In the middle of this mess, God raised up Ezekiel. But Ezekiel is not just one more prophetic player in the lineup to warn about the final demise of Jerusalem. God raised up Ezekiel to help those in exile interpret and deal with these events. Through Ezekiel, God provided a corrective lens to their faulty interpretation of the two Babylonian invasions on Jerusalem (606 BC and 597 BC) and the final blow yet to come (586 BC). The situation back in Jerusalem demanded that the exiles in Babylon be anchored in reality.

It was not a time to doubt or deny the death of the community (Ezek. 12:27), or heed false prophets assuring the community's preservation and who predicted a short exile (Ezek. 13). It was not a time to deny their guilt and pass blame on to others for their suffering (Ezek. 18:1–4), question Yahweh's justice (18:25, 29), or hope for the city's preservation or for the safety of loved ones. It was a time to sigh, groan, mourn, and demonstrate a godly shame for their sins (Ezek. 11:8; 21:6–7, 12; 24:18). "Go through the city of Jerusalem and put a mark on the foreheads of those who grieve and lament over all the detestable things that are done in it," says the Lord to the man clothed in linen in the vision of abandonment (9:4). "But don't touch anyone who has the mark." Based on Ezekiel's own mournful response—"Alas, Sovereign Lord! Are you going to destroy the entire remnant of Israel in this outpouring of your wrath on Jerusalem?" (11:8)—a huge slaughter took place since there were not found in the city those that mourned and grieved over sin.

A bleak picture unfolds. Hardened and theologically weak people have a misplaced hope and lack a sincere, deeply felt sorrow. Back in Jerusalem *and* in Babylon, the people were hardened and could not mourn. They could not respond with the natural and normal sentiment associated with death and death-like circumstances. Hardness and denial led to unnatural emotional responses and incomprehensible questions, which showed a lack of theological acumen.[6] "And when they say to you, 'Why do you groan?' you shall say because of the news that it is coming" (Ezek. 21:7). "Will you not tell us what these things mean for us, that you are acting thus" (24:19)?

*Ezekiel's Portrayal in the Book*

For this reason—the inability of the people to understand and respond emotionally to their sin—Ezekiel takes on the role of a mourner in the book. By eating a scroll containing lamentation, mourning, and woe, Ezekiel becomes what he eats (2:8–9).[7] He describes himself after the incident: "I went bitterly in the fury of my spirit. . . . I came to the exiles. . . . I sat there seven days overwhelmed in their midst" (3:15). Here he tells us that he is filled with strong emotions and that these feelings are consistent with the scroll he swallowed. Both his emotional and physical demeanor point to the fact that he is mourning. His posture of mourning immediately evidences this when he sits in stunned silence for a period of *seven* days in response to eating the scroll (3:15). Seven days is the typical period of mourning. Job and his friends sat for seven days in a stunned silence mourning the events in his life, so too Ezekiel sits in a stunned silence for seven days.

Many of his actions afterward in chapters 4–24 also show that he has become a mourner.[8] For example, his sentence to house confinement and speechlessness that persists until the city falls could indicate an extended morning period (ch. 4). Various commanded gestures such as cutting hair from his beard and head (5:1), clapping hands, stomping feet, and saying "alas" in response to the evil abominations of the house of Israel further indicate mourning (5:1; 6:11). On two occasions, he utilizes words associated with grief and mourning when he asks God to spare Israel from further destruction (9:8–10; 11:13). He mourns for Jerusalem's princes (ch. 19), and he demonstrates mourning for the city of Jerusalem by striking his thigh (21:17). Ezekiel symbolically reenacts Israel's funeral procession and mourns inwardly when his wife dies (21:17; 24:15–24). He even mourns the downfall of the kings of Tyre and Egypt (27–28:19; 32:1–16). In this way, the man became the message and the means by which the exiles should interpret their circumstances.

His role as a mourner is critical given their barriers to mourning, and this role seems to add to his multifaceted role established throughout the book. Ezekiel is portrayed as Israel's prophet (2:5; 33:33), watchman (3:17; 33:7), sign (12:6, 11; 24:24, 27), judge (20:4; 22:2) and funeral director (19:1; 27:1–11, 26–36; 28:11; 32:1). He is Yahweh's "son of man" (e.g., 2:1). As indicated by these multifaceted portrayals, Ezekiel has different functional identities in the book. He role-plays, and a mourner is one of his many roles. Thus Ezekiel "enacts mourning," as it were, for the death of the community since the community deserves the judgment of death through its sin (see also Ezra 9:3–4).

## The Purpose of Lamentation in the Book and Significance of Ezekiel's Mourning Role

What is the purpose and point of Ezekiel becoming a mourner in the midst of the exiles? If "hardened" defines the exiles in Babylon, and if Jerusalem lacks those who mourn, then one begins to understand Ezekiel's purpose here: He mourns as a model of what they should be doing. God's aim through Ezekiel was for the people to lament over their situation *before* the inevitable events of 586 BC. They were to respond to their own sinful situation the way Ezekiel responded when called as a prophet to these hardened people (he mourned)![9]

An attitude of mourning—to sign, to groan, and to be ashamed for their sins—could potentially lead them to acknowledge their wrongdoing (21:6–7, 12–13; 24:18). Though a change of circumstances was not possible even if they did mourn, at least mourning would show a change of heart—and God was after their hearts (18:31; 36:26). This desire for a change in heart demonstrated by Ezekiel's mourning role helps explain the unexpected calls to "repent" in the book.

Ezekiel exhorts his audience on three occasions to do a 180-degree turn (14:6; 18: 30–32; 33:11): to "repent" or "repent and live" (18:32) or "repent and get a new heart and spirit" (18:31) even though the judgment of 586 BC was inevitable. But how and why should Ezekiel's audience "repent"? Indeed, the scroll guaranteed, along with all of Ezekiel's prophecies and dramatic acts, that the judgment of God could not be reversed nor deferred any longer. In other words, the people could not alter their future.

What effect would Ezekiel's mourning role, the repeated messages of inevitable judgment, together with these three calls to repent have on his audience? It would affect the hearers by giving *them* the possibility to examine their hearts and change. God wanted changed hearts and attitudes toward sin, even though a change of consequences and circumstances was not possible. He wanted an admission of guilt, an acknowledgment of wrongdoing. Mourning here does connect to repentance if the latter concerns a changed heart, something eventually leading to a changed lifestyle. Mourning alone, however, could be an alternative to false repentance.[10] But neither mourning nor repentance are preconditions for averting consequences in Ezekiel.

Mourning over sin in Ezekiel 4–24 relative to judgment passages also connects with shame over sin discussed in some of the restoration passages sprinkled throughout the book as Ezekiel unfolds an elaborate picture of restoration for the exiles. Commentators on Ezekiel have correctly observed in several places that the purposes of this future restoration are connected to having a godly shame over past conduct. The Lord says through Ezekiel: " I will restore your fortunes . . . *so that* you may bear your disgrace and be ashamed of what you have done" (16:54); "*Then* when I make atonement for you for all you have done, you will remember and be ashamed" (16:63); "I will cleanse you . . . *then* you will remember your evil ways and wicked deeds, and you will loathe yourselves . . . [and] be ashamed and be disgraced for your conduct (36:31–32); "Son of man, describe the temple *so that* they may be ashamed of their sins" (43:10–11). Thus shame *and* mourning naturally go together when speaking of sentiment over sin in Ezekiel (see also Ezra 9:6–15).

Mourning would be rendered impossible *if*, indeed, mourning, repentance, and shame were preconditions for Israel's restoration. However, as others have also noted, the texts above that reflect attitudes of mourning and shame were not precursors to the restorative acts of Yahweh but the consequences of it (see Ezek. 16:54, 63; 36:31–32; 43:10–11; so too Jer. 31:8–9). This is why God allows Ezekiel to show his audience visions of restoration from many angles in the book (their return from exile, their cleansing and unity, and especially the rebuilt temple; Ezek. 36–37; 40–48). In the fuller description of restoration outlined in Ezekiel 34–48, the stress falls on the efforts and acts of Yahweh who brings about restoration, so that his goodness would lead them to have a change in heart; that is, they would be ashamed after visualizing this restoration. Genuine spiritual transformation involves a heart change from past conduct and is directly tied to restoration (36:31). Thus, Ezekiel's calls to repentance are wake up calls intending to emphasize the exiles' guilt (a huge theme in the book of Ezekiel), an acknowledgement of wrongdoing that was meant to produce a godly grief and shame (see also Jer. 3:13).

Mourning before the promised and predicted judgment of 586 BC shows a heart change. In the same way, shame, after seeing the promised and predicted restoration, shows a heart change. Together, mourning and shame are healthy and necessary emotions for an effective lifestyle change—ones that should be expressed and not repressed. But hard-hearted people, and those in denial, are incapable of either of these emotions. So Ezekiel becomes a mourner in their midst.

We have seen that sin plus judgment results in death and that, ultimately, death brings lamentation because of sin and attitudes of mourning and shame are the heart postures God desires. The main idea of Ezekiel—the theme of death and Ezekiel's portrayal of a mourner—demonstrates the dominant theme of lamentation in the book: yet out of death restored life will come, out of lamentation comes joy, that which was contaminated becomes cleansed, and that which was dead comes back to life. But how? Only the supernatural power of God will enable this. In both death and life, God will receive the glory he desires and deserves.[11] But the development of life coming out of death pertains to a chapter in another book!

## The Pastoral Point of Understanding Lament in Ezekiel

What does Ezekiel teach us about mourning and lamentation? The kind of lamentation that Ezekiel addresses is *not* related to personal loss and tragedy because of life's unexpected curveballs. The lamentation here is grief over sin's consequences.[12]

Like Ezekiel living among the exiles, our task as members of the body of Christ is to help people properly interpret the events and situations of their lives while living out sin's affects. We need to anchor them in reality by giving a biblical interpretive framework for understanding sin's consequences. We must offer correctives to people's faulty interpretations of the messes made of their lives.

Like Ezekiel's audience, generating false ideas about God and his character when suffering sin's consequences seems easier than searching for truth about our character. Statements such as "God is not just" abound. "God will take care of me; I will not get pregnant!" "My wife will never know!" "God will protect me from . . . after all, I still go to church and come from a Christian family." In other words, we want to believe what we want to believe and tend to hold on to hopes that are not theologically grounded. As a result, we experience little to no remorse. We hope and even assume that the consequences will be short-lived or perhaps that there won't be any. We prefer blaming others and typically ask the wrong questions, therefore dodging the real problem of owning our guilt. Barriers abound to mourning sin's consequences.

Ezekiel reminds us that even while living out sin's consequences, people's hearts continue in a hardened posture. We desperately need to understand the position of the human heart (i.e., Jer. 17:9; Mark 7:21). Neutral it is not. The heart is either soft or hard, but never neutral. Rebellious hearts keep rebelling. A hardened heart prohibits remorse for sin. Denial of wrongdoing equates to a denial of the emotion of regret. Denial is deadly and does not produce fruit.

In this regard, Ezekiel teaches us that we should be praying not for God to change people's circumstances necessarily, but praying for God to change hearts in those circumstances. "Get a new heart," Ezekiel says! Getting a new heart this side of the cross remains impossible, except for the transforming work of the Holy Spirit who specializes in turning hearts of stone into hearts of flesh. Because of the regenerating work of the Holy Spirit, we have the power to admit guilt and acknowledge wrongdoing, which produces mourning and godly shame—one that motivates us to action, to do God's will and follow his ways. Together, mourning and shame are healthy and necessary emotions for an effective heart change that leads to a lifestyle change. Mourning and shame are emotions that should be expressed, not repressed.

While we cannot produce these emotions in people hardened by sin's consequences, we can certainly be role models. In this regard, Ezra provides a superb role model—one who does what Ezekiel's audience was incapable of doing. In Ezra 9–10, there is a heartbreaking story. On the heels of getting their lives back together after exile (seeing and experiencing God's goodness to restore them), some of the leaders in the community, among others, were unfaithful to God, which expressed itself in marriages to foreign women. The "holy race" was no longer so holy! They mingled with the peoples around them and intermarried (Ezra 9:2). On hearing this news, Ezra—the minister in residence at the time and the one delivering them the word of God—has an amazing response. He first goes into mourning (9:3-4), confesses shame (9:6), and acknowledges guilt even though he was not among the guilty (see 9:15 especially). With Ezra, there is a clear relationship between lament and confession of sin.[13] His response sparks something in the community: "While Ezra was praying and confessing, weeping and throwing himself down ... a large crowd of Israelites—men, women and children—gathered around him" (10:1). Notice what they did: "They too wept bitterly" (v. 2).

His prayer brought conviction. It emphasized their guilt and acknowledged wrongdoing, producing in Ezra and the people a godly sorrow and shame (9:6, 10; 10:1-2, 12). How could they *not* weep and be ashamed? God had restored their markers of identity by allowing them to return to Jerusalem, rebuild, and reestablish Torah, yet they blew it once again. Years later, Ezra and his audience do what Ezekiel's audience was not capable of doing. In fact, they took radical actions (10:3) in the hope that God would withhold further judgment (9:14). In this case, mourning, shame, and action were all part of the process. They underwent true spiritual transformation, whereby they had a change of heart for their past conduct.

Ezra is a role model. Imagine weeping like Ezra after hearing the news of unfaithfulness of a sister or brother in your congregation? Imagine the kind of revival it might cause. Unfortunately, I can count on only one hand the times I was deeply grieved by sin's consequences in my own sin or in the life of someone I know.

Most of the time, our own response is shock and more of an emotional numbness, which is probably judgmental and critical. I don't think we fully grasp the grief associated with turning aside from God's ways.

We have to learn to lament in this manner. It is easy to proclaim the victory but leave lamenting for sin's consequences aside. In keeping with the purpose of this book and to substantiate a point voiced elsewhere, we contribute to the neglect of lament in the church because of denial and hard hearts. "When I kept silent about my sin I wasted away," says the psalmist (Ps. 32:3–5), and in this regard lamenting *is* better than silence (as has been stated elsewhere by my colleagues).

If, in fact, all creation is groaning, mourning, and lamenting from ongoing human sin and subsequent divine recompense (Rom. 8:22), and if humans groan inwardly as we await adoption to sonship (Rom. 8:23),[14] then it follows that mourning for sin's consequences should be a part of our spiritual routine. It is a time to mourn in this regard. That is to say, while New Testament writers use the Old Testament exile (1 Pet. 1:1–2) or wilderness motifs (Rev. 12) to speak of a Christian's sojourn on this earth, they also incorporate the Old Testament lament motif. Thus, in light of Romans, it seems appropriate to include a posture of mourning over sin as a theological necessity. Until the old order of things passes away, indeed, there are tears in our eyes. Death, mourning, and crying will prevail until the old order of things passes away and we embrace the new (Rev. 21:3–4). Until then, it is a time to mourn.[15]

Finally, Ezekiel teaches us the critical connection between mourning, shame, and restoration. He "sees" restoration through various visions, which were meant to produce remorse and shame. The restoration he envisions for the exiles is supernatural and points us forward in redemptive history so that God allows us to see restoration too. The cross becomes our vision, and we must hold high the cross of Jesus.

Looking to the restoration Jesus offers us should prick and poke at our hearts and cause us to weep, be ashamed, and have changed hearts. How can I keep on doing X when Jesus has given me everything, restored my soul, redeemed me from the pit of hell, given me life everlasting? Or conversely, one could also say, how could I have done X given what Jesus has done? In both situations, a heartfelt change manifests itself, hard hearts become soft, and true remorse for sin surfaces. Like Ezekiel's vision of restoration, the cross is our great visual aide of God's power to restore. This reality should overwhelm us emotionally—not just when we are saved, but over and over again. To use a phrase from one of our other contributors, we "build lament into our résumés" by keeping our eyes on the cross. We have an advocate with the Father, so that when we keep on sinning there is hope! In this regard, the cross must always be before us. As a colleague of mine once said we need to keep "gospel-ing" ourselves. We need to keep "good news-ing" ourselves! This will keep our hearts tender.

God showed up to restore and bring life out of death. Jesus said, "I am the resurrection and the life; he who believes in me, though he die, yet he shall live" (John 11:25). God initiated a supernatural restoration through Jesus. God sent Jesus into our mournful and exile-like circumstances. Jesus was a tangible manifestation of God's grace and mercy to people living in sin's consequences. Jesus is *the* restorative answer to the messes people make of their lives. Jesus is the God-given lens to whom we must cling for the hope of restoration. Because Jesus incorporated lament into his life our mourning turns to joy. Out of death restored life will come! Out of lamentation comes joy. That which was contaminated is cleansed. That which was dead produces fruit. But how? Through the supernatural power of God. One day, as the song based on Isaiah goes, "we will feast in the house of Zion; we will sing with our hearts restored. He has done great things and we will say together, *we will feast and weep no more!*"

He will swallow up death forever, the sovereign Lord will wipe away the tears from all faces; he will remove his people's disgrace from all the earth. The Lord has spoken (Isa. 25:6–7).

# 3

## LAMENT AMONG EVANGELICALS: HISTORICAL REFLECTIONS ON PASTORAL PRACTICE

### Rhys S. Bezzant

*The Book of Mormon* is one of the most highly rated musicals in recent memory and, despite its crudities, gives evangelical Christians a profound insight into contemporary missiology. A group of recently minted Mormon missionaries head out from Salt Lake City to their assigned destination, Uganda, for two years of service. However, they find that their training in intercultural skills is still lacking. They look for a doorbell on a small African hut but then remember how to knock. They struggle to know how to deal with warlords and AIDS, and don't immediately get any conversions leading to baptisms. One of them fantasizes about his dream ministry destination, Orlando. In the musical, we note the distance between the missionaries and their hearers. But the more disturbing disconnect for me was between the characters and the audience. When the missionaries—crisply dressed and well spoken—offered a life of ease and a source of power, the audience did not side with them but with the dispossessed, confused, and apparently powerless Africans. The biggest missiological challenge for the Mormons appeared to be how to get into the shoes of those who were suffering. Elder Price—a handsome, capable success story—flees at the first sign of danger, unprepared for service in a land of suffering. Weakness had no place in his résumé.

It is my aim here to help us see that we evangelicals are a lot more like Elder Price than we recognize. One of the most significant reasons why evangelicals find it hard to lament is because as a movement we have failed to recognize how drunk we are on power and how allergic we are to weakness. There may be many personal influences that make such honesty difficult; but it is certainly the case that over the last three hundred years evangelicalism, for reasons good and bad, has had a contested relationship with power and weakness. If we need to learn how to lament in a biblical way, then we might first have to learn how to be powerless. To call out to God with desperate appeals for rescue, to express deep frustration over our plight in praying "How long, O Lord?" and to have nowhere to go but to God with our feelings of frustration, is to confess to being powerless, and to ask for God's intervention. When we lament, we acknowledge weakness as part of our story.

I won't attempt to trace tight lines of cause and effect between historical turning points and contemporary spirituality, but more impressionistically show that at significant moments in the evangelical movement context has shaped evangelicals, such that we have chosen power over weakness. We need to see the bigger pressures shaping our movement if we are to strive against them, and so engage evangelistically more honestly with the audience members at *The Book of Mormon*, who were very open to owning lament as a significant feature of their lives.

## Birth of the Movement: The Power of Godliness in the Eighteenth-Century Revivals

The relationship of Christians with power is as old as the Christian movement itself. Paul's converts in Corinth were beguiled by it, and Christians living in the time of Emperor Constantine after an age of persecution were relieved when they received it. After the fall of the Roman Empire, the church took up new responsibilities in terms of secular power, and in time the clergy saw themselves exercising power by virtue of their ordination through the means of the seven sacraments. The laity became passive observers, no longer active participants, in the life of the church, seeking out power and control of their environment instead through superstitious rituals. Drawing on the vocabulary of Romans 1, the sixteenth-century Reformers sought out a new kind of power for salvation announced in the gospel, which would provide assurance and ultimately mobilize the laity.[1]

Modern evangelicalism has its clearest birth, however, in the revivals of the eighteenth century, which drew on the resources of the Reformation but gave them a new shape and importance in a world colored by Enlightenment norms and values.[2] In the context of a nominally Protestant church, believers (often on the margins of the institutional church) expressed resistance to compromised and ossified hierarchies through preaching the new birth and encouraging new, more agile networks and structures for mission. Reginald Ward has drawn our attention to the apparently random emergence of these new kinds of piety in the long eighteenth century among Salzburg and Bristol miners, among Lutherans in the militaristic Prussian state, or on the edge of the British Empire in Savannah or Northampton.[3] He argues that in places where churches were under pressure, part of their political, economic, or spiritual resistance was to pursue an anti-assimilationist spirituality and find empowerment for those suffering under social, political, and ecclesiastical duress. One of the leading slogans of the eighteenth-century revivals—whether Methodist, Congregationalist, or Pietist—was to summarize their protest in the words "the power of godliness," picking up on what the apostle Paul writes in 2 Timothy 3:5, where he decries those in the church who spoke of the importance of godliness but denied its power.

In addition to their context, another significant influence on the revivalists was the Enlightenment, which radically broke with the traditional claims of institutional religion, highlighting instead the power of personal agency available through individual rationality. The challenge given by Immanuel Kant was to dare to believe in one's own majority, or mature capacity, to make decisions without reference to received authority. This overlay gave extra intensity to the doctrine of regeneration—itself a metaphor loaded with the sentiment of power, fresh beginnings, and individual agency. Listen to these eighteenth-century voices praise the presence of power in their lives:

> *George Whitefield*: "For the world being now become nominally Christian, at least (though, God knows, little of the power is left among us), there need not outward miracles, but only an inward cooperation of the Holy Spirit with the word to prove that Jesus is that Messiah which was to come into the world."
>
> *Thomas Walsh*: "I look for religion to possess, and entirely to change me. I see and feel that Christianity is something divine, living, generous, powerful, and internal. It is God dwelling in the soul of a person."
>
> *John Witherspoon*: "Suffer me to beseech you, or rather to give you warning not to rest satisfied with a form of godliness, denying the power thereof."
>
> *Sarah Osborn*: "My soul said, it is good for me to be here [at the Supper]. I was enabled, with all my powers engaged, to renew my dedication of myself to God, and rejoice in my choice of him."[4]

It has been recognized as well that one of the leading interpreters of the eighteenth-century revivals, Jonathan Edwards, understood the art of preaching not in terms of beauty or reason, but in terms of power. As a wordsmith, Edwards used his skills in rhetoric to create a powerful impact on listeners in his homiletic ministry.[5] Form and content should mesh: if preaching about the power of regeneration, the sermon's shape and texture should eloquently reflect the content being presented. Interestingly, Edwards is happy to preach sermons of lament about the state of the nation. These sermons, known as jeremiads, were a common tool in Puritan preaching, in which the preacher despaired of the people's practical piety and exhorted them to a change of belief and behavior. What must be noticed, however, is that though Edwards calls on the people to lament and repent of their sins, he does not honestly expect much response from them. In his sermon "The Dangers of Decline" (1730), he urges the people of Northampton, with him, to "lament our degeneracies and deadness in the things of religion," but he doesn't really expect any response. He writes that "God may leave us to be deceived, and infatuated, and not to understand the things that make for our peace."[6] We know that among other revivalists, John Wesley does at least preach from a psalm of lament; but he dismisses lamenting as faithlessness and instead encourages the believer to look beyond painful circumstances to the possibility of assurance, which is available when one believes in a God of faithfulness.[7]

## Building the Nation: Powerful Preachers in the Second Great Awakening

The American Revolution marked a watershed in the understanding and practice of evangelical faith. Though the language of sovereignty was embedded in the Great Awakening of the eighteenth century, this very same vocabulary was repurposed in revolutionary politics to apply to the nature of the people and the republic they maintained. There was a shift in power away from the vested interests of the Crown and Parliament of the United Kingdom and the clerical establishment of the New World toward the rights and duties of the people in the new democratic republic of the United States. Authority was understood now to reside in the mass of the people, not in elite leadership. Andrew Jackson, the populist politician, clearly responded to this transfer of power to the common people.

However, among evangelicals—those tracing their roots back to the populism and protest and priorities of the leaders of the First Great Awakening—there was a reflex reaction to the social arrangements of the new nation. The deistic assumptions of many of the founders, and the need to secure order where social authority was no longer vested in the elite, gave to the churches new responsibilities and identity. The demand for the church to provide a moral citizenry, and the capacity of the leadership of the church to exercise moral authority, were both contested. The clergy, and preaching pastors in particular, sought to win back power for the sake of the gospel's advance. Democratization of the nation, as Nathan Hatch has observed, led to new practices, such as emotional preaching or altar calls, in order to more directly impact deistic unbelief in the cities or theistic backsliders on the frontier.[8] This was not the moment to encourage the feelings of powerless lament, but to centralize power afresh in clerical ministrations of the Second Great Awakening, whether among Yale undergraduates, farmers in upstate New York, or homesteaders on the Kentucky frontier.

Charles Finney—a Presbyterian revivalist whose base was New York but who moved to Ohio—set about mechanizing and regularizing the processes of revival, suggesting that the conversions of large numbers of people should not be surprising but rather predictable when certain means were applied and sentiments cultivated. This was the efficient use of powerful methods to secure certain results. Although his strategy was designed to appeal to people outside of the normal routine of church life, his approach to ministry profoundly impacted regular church life as well. Sunday services more and more took on the characteristics of revival meetings, which had no place for lament but which were designed to promote the power of the gospel packaged in powerful idioms of music and oratory. No longer were church services designed to exercise several spiritual muscles, with lament among them, but now one central spiritual muscle was given a workout—namely, our capacity to make a decision for Christ, normally toward the end of the meeting, with an invitation to take the sawdust trail to the front of the meeting space. Many, if not most, evangelical church services today still follow the same template. No psalms are used, however, because there is no fixed calendar of scriptural readings.

The practices of revivalist evangelism drew on the categories of Enlightenment machine-like predictability, but they also drew on the emotional strand of sentimentality, which was at home in the cultural mood of Romanticism (transcendentalism in the American context), and comfortable with the Common Sense Realism that was birthed in eighteenth-century Scotland but found deep root in nineteenth-century evangelicalism. It was also nurtured in domestic settings. At heart, sentimentalism believed that moral action was generated by moral feeling—something not possessed by elites alone, but by any human agent.[9] Such feelings of sentimentality could reduce feelings of pain or distaste by "selecting and editing memories to present them in a form that avoids recognition of unpleasantness," and ultimately morphs into a kind of narcissism, in which "clear engagement with the difficulties of human life" was avoided.[10] Universality was no longer defined in terms of rationality, but in terms of sentimentality common to all with a heart. It was literature in this mold, such as *Uncle Tom's Cabin*, that generated concern for social amelioration and abolition in particular.

Connected to themes of sentimentality is the practice of hymnody, the chief operating strategy to affirm and transmit evangelical spirituality. If you are going to highlight the theological distinctive of regeneration, the best way is to sing about it, not to write a creed to define it. Popular religion after the Second Great Awakening was identified by "hierophanic transformation of the soul by the sovereign power of God."[11] This phrase points us to the belief that God was expected to intervene dramatically in the common life of believers, and thereby it defended musically the belief that God wants to be close to us. Indeed, the lyrics of many hymns of the day did not provide a full range of theological topics or spiritual dispositions, but ones that instead talked about God's power in personal salvation or in cosmic triumph. Rather than struggling to find words to call out to God in stuttering lament, a person could manage to find a thousand tongues to sing our great Redeemer's praise. God's universal accessibility is honored when we sing:

> O Lord, my God, when I in awesome wonder
> Consider all the worlds Thy Hands have made
> I see the stars, I hear the rolling thunder
> Thy power throughout the universe displayed.[12]

However, the powerful experience of praise, which in a world where God's absence was increasingly assumed was profoundly encouraging, could nonetheless diminish the possibility of lament. The turn to Arminian theological categories in this new world of free decision-making, borne along by the successes of Methodism on the frontier, reinforced not Calvinist determinism but Arminian personal agency and baptized the pursuit of power, even if within limits.

## Belief in Holiness: Power of Purity in the Thought of the Gilded Age

After the American Civil War (1861–1865), doctrine seemed to have less hold on the majority of the population, for Christians—north and south—believed they had been fighting according to God's will. Certainly, Reformed faith was less potent and Arminian categories espousing free will were preached, not least in African-American churches. Methodist commitment to scriptural holiness caught the attention of the nation, a kind of piety that could be promoted by lay leadership and that encouraged escape from the world of politics. Perfectibility, always a category in Wesley's teaching, found a new home in the Gilded Age. This was distinctly not a spirituality that encouraged lament, but was one that optimistically believed in the power of progress. D. L. Moody was the pin-up boy of this new age, in which the wealthy were targets of evangelism and their conversion validated the power of Christian preaching. One of Moody's greatest spiritual dangers was his "ambition to lead and influence rich men."[13]

The power of progress was birthed in an environment of industrialization, urbanization, mass migration, technological innovation, and scientific discovery in the United States in the second half of the nineteenth century. Afraid of the emasculating influence of factories, in which men were no longer needed for their physical strength, Christians got behind movements, such as the Young Men's Christian Association (YMCA) and ultimately the repristinated Olympic Games, to encourage men to exercise and build healthy bodies despite the squalor of their living conditions or the toxicity of their work environment. A movement known as Muscular Christianity emerged, not just in the US but elsewhere in

Europe and Australasia, which linked physical strength to religious certainty and individual capacity to control a world that felt more and more uncertain and overpowering.[14] Perhaps this was also a reaction to the emergence of the domestic ideal in the Victorian age, which had made female piety to be one of the highest expressions of Christian devotion. Military and athletic metaphors abounded, not least in hymns, and Billy Sunday, the earliest twentieth-century evangelist, appealed in this way to men to give their lives to Christ:

> Many think a Christian has to be a sort of dishrag proposition, a wishy-washy, sissified sort of galoot that lets everybody make a doormat out of him. . . . Let me tell you the manliest man is the man who will acknowledge Jesus Christ.[15]

Though masculinity can be shaped in different ways in different contexts, in this instance as well as others, it represented "an impulse to impose order on a world widely perceived as chaotic, and to provide identity, direction, and solidarity."[16] Lament is unlikely to take deep root in a culture that rejects "sissified" religion.

This period also witnessed a theological transition from a church that espoused postmillennialism, to one in which premillennialism became the norm. Though economic conditions had deteriorated, evangelical Christians were less likely to be advocates for social engagement or amelioration. There was plenty to lament, but it was not the reflex reaction in much of the spirituality of the day. Instead, an apocalyptic sensibility took deep root, acknowledging human powerlessness and the need of divine intervention to set things straight; but this was coupled with dispensationalism, which set up history into a series of epochs, each representing a particular divine strategy of engagement. If history felt out of control, then perhaps some measure of security could be found in working out where God was up to in his own plans for the cosmos. Turning to the maths of millenarianism gave to eschatological investigators a sense of control in the long term at least. White Protestant evangelical hegemony was under threat, but power to understand God's plans and the place of individual regeneration within them was a tonic nonetheless.[17] Further, the gradualism and anti-supernaturalism inherent to Darwinian theories of causation, and the reaction to revivalism in Bushnell's advocacy of the importance of Christian nurture, made dispensationalism a fitting protest to modern notions of divine engagement with the world.

A more obscure feature of late nineteenth-century life that bears on our topic has been outlined by Kate Bowler in her book *Blessed*. Her goal is to explain the rise of the prosperity gospel, which could guarantee "a special form of Christian power to reach into God's treasure trove and pull out a miracle."[18] In this movement, spiritual realities can be read off material conditions, whether health, wealth, or victory. In particular, she introduces the reader to the evangelist E. W. Kenyon and his idealist philosophy of "New Thought," which described a type of mind power that enabled human perfectibility, drawing down the tropes of holiness movements. In essence, this was a theory of causation that made appeal to invisible but powerful forces in the universe. This was, after all, the era in which germ theory had been developed. Furthermore, just as God created the world by the power of his speech, so Christians could access power through the spoken word to secure, by faith, God's material blessings. Calling on the name of Jesus "held forensic significance."[19] In time, speaking in tongues became another way to access these kinds of power too. Science and its possibilities, alongside holiness traditions and idealist philosophy of the mind, enabled a new kind of power religion.

## Blessed Assurance: The Right Side of Power in World Wars and Cold War

A common assumption about the beginning of the twentieth century is that conservative evangelicals withdrew from culture to defend traditional doctrine over against the Social Gospellers, or liberal varieties of the faith. They became known as fundamentalists when they published a series of essays espousing conservative beliefs under the title *The Fundamentals* (1910–1915). In time, recognizing that they had not stopped moral and theological decline, so the story goes, they reengaged with the mainstream in 1942 with the construction of the National Association of Evangelicals, choosing the more traditional epithet for their organization. In this telling of the story, the primary distinctive of evangelicals in the late nineteenth century was their anti-modernism, but this is probably only one part of the story.

Another way of telling the story is not so much that evangelicals were against modernity, but rather that they had become increasingly apocalyptic, seeing their movement as eschatologically shaped rather than merely philosophically reactive. To be responsive to the apocalyptic themes of the Bible is to see the church's need for the intervention of God in power, though not in the meantime necessarily passive in the face of the world. A motto among many of them was "Occupy until I come," picking up the phrasing from the KJV of Luke 19:13, in which the master of the parable advises those charged with his finances to invest his money, or engage in business, until his return. Waiting for the Lord doesn't mean disengagement from society or lamenting mournfully but "constant action."[20] Fundamentalists and/or apocalyptic evangelicals were not as passive as has been thought.

Furthermore, although the US came to World War I later than the European powers, the impact of the Great War was felt even before 1917, for it was itself an almost apocalyptic event with empires collapsing and warfare on a scale not before known with monstrous technological possibilities. Breaking free from its isolationism, the US asked much of its citizens; and fundamentalists, rather than withdrawing, offered themselves in service for the bigger cause of democracy. Their antipathy toward German higher criticism of the Bible may have fueled their righteous anger and reinforced their nationalist pride. Pentecostals actively organized themselves into denominations in this period,[21] and the fall of the Ottoman Empire made space for fresh thinking about the role of Israel in God's geopolitical purposes. WWI was not only "Great" but it was also "Holy," superimposed with the theology of premillennialism and the piety of power: "The war had transformed what might otherwise have remained a somewhat obscure theological conviction on the fringes of Protestant life into a major force."[22] There was much to lament in terms of the loss of life, but being on the side of victory in cosmic battle could assuage feelings of powerlessness and shore up the experience of weakness.

The years after WWI were ones in which evangelicals turned to build the infrastructure of a subculture. With publishing houses, Bible colleges, campsites, seminaries, new denominations, missions societies, and serious wealth underscoring their achievements, this was a movement that was not content to remain disengaged. New communication technologies such as radio were harnessed for evangelistic purposes, and revival tents with powerful itinerant evangelists traveled from town to town. The Bolshevik Revolution of 1917 became the backdrop for evangelical rhetoric, which saw the world in stark and oppositional terms. The gospel was aligned with the successes of capitalism, shown in two world wars to be the most powerful of economic systems. Though Billy Graham started out as a youth worker and local evangelist, his life coincided with the tumultuous events of the twentieth century: born in the year in which WWI ended, supporting presidents in their tough political decisions, preaching against the evils of the Soviet Empire, acting as emissary for the US government behind the Iron Curtain in soft diplomacy, caught up in protests about the Vietnam War, and as a Southerner necessarily involved in debates concerning the Civil Rights Movement. He was friend to twelve sitting presidents and had his fingers burnt when he naively supported Richard Nixon before his resignation in 1974.[23] He no doubt felt that he was fulfilling his patriotic duty to engage in political life as he did, but it could also be argued that he succumbed not to the sins of money or sex but to the desire for power. As Grant Wacker has said, "Perennially hobnobbing with the rich and the famous, Graham seemed to represent not only Establishment Evangelicalism but also Establishment America."[24] Or, "Proximity to him became proximity to normative authority."[25] There were, of course, very particular reasons why Graham's life took the course it did. But it must be acknowledged as well that he inhabited a longer evangelical story and reinforced that story's strengths and weaknesses in his own biography. He is an icon of twentieth-century evangelicalism.

The growth of Pentecostalism in the course of the twentieth century should not go unrecognized in this brief survey. Its power is seen in its reach and resistance to much of modern Western norms, and its power is also more overtly preached. Ecstatic utterance might demonstrate spiritual gifts and prophesying demonstrate verbal power. John Wimber in the latter half of the century espoused power religion and power encounters, drawing on revivalist models, supernaturalist eschatology, and cultural assumptions of power and weakness. The power of the gospel was as much a depiction of geographic advance in the book of Acts as it was a theological assumption in the book of Romans. The Cold War might be over, but the spiritual war never ends.

## Buttressing Resistance: Power Dynamics in the Post-Christian Age

This survey of the attraction of power in the evangelical tradition comes to us as a warning. It is certainly part of our DNA as believers who want to preach and experience the new birth. But we must not deny that the language of power is written throughout the entire New Testament. The Holy Spirit brings to us the divine life and cannot leave us the same. New birth empowers our discipline and motivates our obedience. Resurrection from the dead, for Christ and then for us, requires power in our innermost being, according to the apostle Paul in Ephesians 1.

However, there is also in our story an allergic reaction at almost every point to feelings of powerlessness. Perhaps because our story is so closely aligned with the development of personal agency in the modern world, or perhaps because from the earliest days the influence of deism and ultimately secularism has pushed supernatural faith to the edges of society, we seem not to have been able to embed lament in our liturgies, or pieties, or stories. Indeed, as

Robert Calwell said in an interview concerning his book *Theologies of the American Revivalists: From Whitefield to Finney*,

> Evangelicals tend to identify with a strong, powerful leaders who preach the gospel with passion and clarity—men like Whitefield, Moody, and/or Graham. This is still with us today; just notice how many evangelical subgroups are built not so much around the ministry of the Word but upon the foundation of a personality, either an evangelist, a pastor, a blogger, or a conference speaker. Depending upon who the person is, this can either be a good thing or a bad thing.[26]

But I fear that nudging up alongside persons of power will not serve us well in the dawning of the post-Christian West. In fact, we will need to accept a position of being without cultural power, and lament can help us in this. My suggestions for learning to lament are as follows:

1. Every so often organize a lament service for your church, in which your people can practice seeing the world through different eyes; we need to make sure our intercessions regularly own and interpret the violence and meaninglessness of our world.

2. Include in your worship each week a song that names sin, suffering, and evil, even if only in one verse or refrain, or occasionally ask a singer to perform a spiritual that owns the experience of powerlessness.

3. Learn to see ourselves and our lives as essentially integrated, with every part connected to every other part, which allows our feelings of abandonment or torment to be acceptable parts of our whole being.

4. Ministers should allow for some vulnerability in their own ministry and to stand with those suffering, which itself creates a culture of honesty essential to the practice of lament

5. Part of the job of the pastor is to provide words to explain feelings or encounters, so this belongs to moments of lament too, perhaps with the use of psalms.

6. Having learned to lament, we exercise one of the most important spiritual muscles of all—learning to be good losers—which comes out of humility as well as sorrow.

In our world, missiology requires lament. Just ask Elder Price.

# 4

# LAMENT IN THE NEW TESTAMENT

Sean M. McDonough

"Rejoice in the Lord always—again I say, rejoice!"
(Phil. 4:4)[1]

Verses such as these are treasured pieces of wisdom for Christians.[2] Far from being isolated bits of encouragement, they sit at the heart of the New Testament witness to Jesus' triumph over the world—a triumph he graciously shares with his people. So the question arises: In the midst of all this victory, is any place left for lament? Or should lament be respectfully laid to rest alongside animal sacrifices, purity laws, and other defunct Old Testament practices?[3]

## The Old Testament Is the Bible of the Early Church

We must begin with a simple but essential point: What we call the Old Testament *was* the Bible of the early church. For the first few decades after Jesus, there were no "New Testament" documents at all; and for the next few decades, a given church would have only a trickle of documents available as letters circulated and Gospels were written and distributed. The Old Testament was not like the first stages of a lunar rocket, dropping off into the ocean once the gospel module reached a sufficient altitude. Rather, the Old Testament was the foundation upon which the witness of the church was established.[4]

Yes, there was a new covenant inaugurated by Jesus that necessitated a rethinking of the sacrificial system, the status of Gentiles, and a host of other issues relating to the specifics of the Sinai Covenant. If nothing else, the advent of Jesus brought a new angle of vision to the interpretation of the Old Testament. But even this new angle of vision had to be justified *from within the Old Testament itself*. Thus texts broadly related to "new covenant" themes (e.g., Jer. 31:31ff.; Isa. 40–66; Ezek. 34; Ps. 110, etc.) formed the textual basis for the proclamation of the early church.

We can affirm as a basic principle, then, that the Old Testament remained formative for the early church, even as its reading strategy departed from other early Jewish counterparts. While many books received widespread attention (for example, Genesis, Exodus, Isaiah, and Daniel), the Psalms would have been a particularly important resource. The Psalms are referenced or alluded to throughout the New Testament, and they would have naturally played a formative role in early Christian worship alongside newly minted Christian hymns.[5] Thus the relative absence of extended, newly minted lament texts does not necessarily reflect the worship practice of New Testament believers. We will examine lament in the New Testament under the assumption they could avail themselves of Old Testament resources to give expression to their struggles.

## The Centrality of Suffering in the Early Church

The Old Testament, then, including its many laments, was available as a resource for the church should it encounter lamentable situations. Here we meet a second and more obvious point, but one that still needs stating: The church did indeed suffer profoundly, even after the triumphant resurrection of Jesus.

This would not have come as a surprise to the apostles. The Gospels record Jesus declaring that suffering was to be an inescapable part of their life:

"Because of this, God in his wisdom said, 'I will send them prophets and apostles, some of whom they will kill and others they will persecute.'" (Luke 11:49)

"All this I have told you so that you will not fall away. They will put you out of the synagogue; in fact, the time is coming when anyone who kills you will think they are offering a service to God." (John 16:1–2)

"I have told you these things, so that in me you may have peace. In this world you will have trouble. But take heart! I have overcome the world." (John 16:33)

The apostles in turn instructed their people in the same truth. After being stoned, Paul "strengthened the disciples and encouraged them" with the words, "We must go through many hardships to enter the kingdom of God" (Acts 14:22). James begins his epistle by telling his people, "Consider it pure joy, my brothers and sisters, whenever you face trials of many kinds" (James 1:2). Peter likewise says, "Dear friends, do not be surprised at the fiery ordeal that has come on you to test you, as though something strange were happening to you" (1 Pet. 4:12).

The assurance of suffering hardly nullified the apostles' confidence in Christ's lordship. Indeed, many of the passages about suffering, such as the texts in James and 1 Peter above, instruct the saints to *rejoice* in the midst of it. Any putative lamentation by early Christians would therefore stand in a paradoxical relationship with the triumph they enjoyed in Jesus. But there is no question that they would have endured countless situations in which lament might be one appropriate response. It remains to demonstrate that they did at times respond in this way, with the full approval of Jesus and the apostles.[6]

## Lament in the Synoptic Gospels

A cursory look at the Synoptic Gospels might suggest that they begin with joy, moving toward lament only in the passion narrative, and that this lament is rather quickly overturned by the joy of the resurrection. While there may be something to that, we must not ignore the sorrow that punctuates the life of Jesus. Amid the generally jubilant tone of Luke's infancy narratives, for instance, we also have sober notes sounded. The fact that Joseph and Mary can find no proper place for the birth of Jesus gives us our first hint that the one who brings the welcome of God will find no welcome on earth. Simeon's words to Mary (Luke 2:34–35) likewise contain a cryptic warning: "This child is destined to cause the falling and rising of many in Israel, and to be a sign that will be spoken against, so that the thoughts of many hearts will be revealed. And a sword will pierce your own soul too." The foreshadowed rejection of Jesus by his countrymen will take dramatic form at the very beginning of his public ministry, as his fellow villagers in Nazareth attempt to throw him off a cliff (Luke 4:29). Lament comes into plain view in Matthew's account in which he records the slaughter of the innocent following the birth of Jesus, interpreting this event through the words of the prophet Jeremiah (Matt. 2:17–18):

"A voice is heard in Ramah,
    weeping and great mourning,
Rachel weeping for her children
    and refusing to be comforted,
because they are no more."

The lamentation for the slain is genuine, but it also serves to foreshadow the lamentable fate of Jesus that awaits. Jesus is depicted as under consistent threat from the religious authorities and even his own townspeople. While he typically does not bewail this situation aloud during his public ministry, we may get a glimpse of something like lament in terse statements such as, "Foxes have dens and birds have nests, but the Son of Man has no place to lay his head" (Luke 9:58).

Lament likewise surfaces in the stories of the desperate people Jesus encounters throughout his public ministry. These instances are particularly important, since they were likely meant to instruct early Christian believers in their own approach to Jesus. The stories not only tell of the wondrous deeds the Messiah did in the past, but they also offer models of faithful supplication in the present—models that include lament at the heart of the experience.[7] An obvious example is the widow in Nain, grieving for her only son. Jesus' first response is heartfelt compassion, as he participates in some measure with her grievous situation. Only then does he offer the exhortation "Do not cry" and raise her son to life.[8] The story of Jairus's daughter later in Luke does not include an explicit statement about Jesus' compassion, but it does feature a common element from the lament psalms: the presence of derisive enemies, here (ironically) in the persons of the presumably professional mourners who mock Jesus' statement that the little girl is only asleep (Luke 8:53).[9]

Perhaps the most dramatic instance of such "enacted lament" comes in the story of the Canaanite woman who asks Jesus to deliver her daughter from demon possession. Gail O'Day demonstrates that the story bears several essential traits of lament: We have an initial invocation, a plea for mercy, an elaboration of the complaint, and an exhortation to action.[10] We may well compare the Canaanite mother's persistent pleading with the psalmists of old and even the Ur-lamenter Job. Stories like these indicate that genuine Christian hope does not rest on the untroubled assumption that there is "a better life to come," but rather in a raw trust in the unaccountable creative power of God to bring life out of death.[11]

## Lament in the Synoptic Passion Accounts

As Jesus' passion draws near, the theme of lament becomes increasingly visible. In Matthew 23:37 (cf. Luke 13:34), Jesus offers a formal lament over the city of Jerusalem: "Jerusalem, Jerusalem, you who kill the prophets and stone those sent to you, how often I have longed to gather your children together, as a hen gathers her chicks under her wings, and you were not willing!" The echoes of the prophetic city laments are deliberate, as Jesus is not merely grieving over his personal rejection, but he also sees the doom of the city drawing near: "Behold, your house is forsaken and desolate" (Matt. 23:38).[12]

In a certain respect, Jesus' lament is preparatory for the reactions to the dread events that will attend his return. Some ascribe the woes to the imminent destruction of Jerusalem, and others to the ultimate end of all things; but in any case, his coming is marked by lament: "Then will appear in heaven the sign of the Son of Man, and then all the tribes of the earth will mourn, and they will see the Son of Man coming on the clouds of heaven with power and great glory" (Matt. 24:30 ESV).

As Rebekah Eklund and others have noted, Jesus' anguish in Gethsemane can profitably be viewed through the lens of lament.[13] Jesus overtly grieves over his situation (see esp. Matt. 26:37–8); indeed, some manuscripts of Luke report that Jesus is in such agony that he sweats drops of blood (Luke 22:43–4). Jesus then lays hold of the lament psalm 42 to express his overwhelming sadness: "My soul is sorrowful to the point of death."[14] The expected presence of enemies, subtly hinted at in episodes like that of Jairus's daughter, now takes on a terrifying sharpness in the presence of soldiers and the ill-intending magistrates who have sent them. The knife twists deeper with the recognition that this, to some extent, was engineered by his friend Judas and that his best friends, including Peter, will betray him. Jesus ultimately resolves to take the cup of suffering and entrust himself into the hands of God; but as Eklund sagely notes, "This relinquishment . . . only comes after the struggle of lament and petition."[15]

The laments of Jesus reach their crescendo in Matthew and Mark in the cry of dereliction on the cross: "My God, my God, why have you forsaken me?" (Matt. 27:46; Mark 15:34).[16] Like so much in the passion narrative, these words come from Psalm 22. It has been duly noted that the psalm begins with lament and ends in hope. This has suggested to some commentators that the dominant note here is Jesus' trust in God, and that the citation of Psalm 22:2 is meant only to point us toward the confident tone of the text's positive denouement. This seems to be an overreach. One can affirm that Jesus maintains his ultimate trust in God, while simultaneously experiencing the anguish of human Godforsakenness.[17] Karl Barth brilliantly captures the theological intent of the cry of dereliction:

But the self-humiliation of God in His Son is genuine and actual, and therefore there is no reservation in respect of His solidarity with us. He did become—and this is the presupposition of all that follows—the brother of man, threatened with man, harassed and assaulted with him, with him in the stream which hurries downwards to the abyss, hastening with him to death, to the cessation of being and nothingness. With him He cries—knowing far better than any other how much reason there is to cry: "My God, my God, why hast thou forsaken me?" (Mk. 15:34). *Deus pro nobis* means simply that God has not abandoned the world and man in the unlimited need of his situation, but that He willed to bear this need as His own, that He took it upon Himself, and that He cries with man in this need.[18]

## John's Gospel

The theme of lament forms an important component of John's Gospel as well. Already in 2:17, after the action in the temple, John refers to a lament from the Psalms: "Zeal for your house will consume me" (Ps. 69:9). This is clearly pointing toward the suffering that Jesus will endure at the end of the Gospel. The point is reinforced by further references to the psalm in the Upper Room discourse (John 15:25, "They hated me without reason," from Ps. 69:4) and the narrative of the crucifixion (John 19:28, where the wine vinegar given to Jesus resonates with Ps. 69:21).

One of the most poignant examples of lament in the entirety of the Scriptures comes in the brief description of Jesus' action before the tomb of Lazarus (11:35): "Jesus wept." Precisely why he is weeping has occasioned much discussion. Those who take the verb ἐνεβριμήσατο in its sense of "to be angry" or "to censure" can see his tears as evincing distress at the unbelief of the villagers in Bethany. While this cannot be dismissed out of hand, one should also note that the companion verb in verse 34, "troubled," is a leitmotif in John's passion and refers more generally to Jesus' distress at his coming death. It is safest to say that the whole situation has moved him to tears: death has ravaged the lives of his good friends; the people around are unable to grasp the magnitude of his power to deliver; and in Lazarus' tomb, he sees what awaits him in a few short days. For our purposes, the fact of Jesus' weeping is more important than its source. A Christian refusing to practice lament would appear to be renouncing the example of Jesus himself.

As Jesus draws near to "the hour" of his death in John, he gives voice to his troubles in the moving soliloquy in 12:27–8: "Now my soul is troubled, and what shall I say? 'Father, save me from this hour'? No, it was for this very reason I came to this hour. Father, glorify your name!" The word for "troubled" here is the same verb as in 11:34, and the expression "my soul [or sometimes 'heart'] is troubled" is a regular feature of the lament psalms (e.g., Ps. 6:4; 37:11; 41:7; 54:5; 108:22; 142:4).

Jesus' final words on the cross in John, "It is finished" (19:30), are likely a note of triumph as he completes the re-creative work he has been about since the Gospel started.[19] Just prior to that, however, his human vulnerability surfaces in his statement, "I thirst" (19:28). In a Gospel drenched with water imagery, these words bring out a characteristically Johannine irony: The one who provides the very water of life (4:10; 7:37–39) lacks the water to sustain his own existence. More pointedly, this very lack embodies the sacrifice that will enable his people to drink the water of eternal life. What is most noteworthy for us is the fact that Jesus here draws upon the lament tradition of the Old Testament. He is most likely invoking Psalm 69 (69:3, "my throat is parched"; 69:21 "they . . . gave me vinegar for my thirst"), with possible resonance from Psalms 22:15, 42:2, and 63:1.[20] As in the Gospels of Matthew and Mark, lament marks Jesus to the end.

## Summary of the Gospels

As a general rule, Jesus in the Gospels does both what we *cannot* do and what we *must* do. He alone successfully overcomes the wiles of the devil, he does mighty deeds incomparable in multitude and magnificence, and his faithfulness culminates in his death on the cross that uniquely takes away the sins of the world. At the same time, he is clearly held forth as an example for all disciples. For this reason, Jesus' open distress at his looming crucifixion can be taken as a model for our own experience of suffering. He does not push aside his sorrow and act as if everything is just fine. He instead pours out his soul in anguish, even as he entrusts himself to the good purposes of God.

If such an *imitatio Christi* seems too daunting (though here we are invited to imitate him in his vulnerability, not his divine power), we may at least take heart from the lamenters who populate the Gospel narratives. As living embodiments of the Old Testament lament psalms, they petition God's representative for deliverance, sometimes overcoming an apparent lack of response through persistent prayer. They find in Jesus a compassionate co-lamenter, as well as a strong hand to release them from their bondage.

## A Sampling of Lament from the Remainder of the New Testament

### *The Apostle Paul*

The book of Romans has long been a touchstone for theology in the Western tradition. It also proves a surprisingly useful point of departure for the investigation of lament in the New Testament outside the Gospels. Romans 7:24 may or may not count as the first instance of Christian lament in the book when someone (but who?) cries out, "What a wretched man I am! Who will rescue me from this body that is subject to death?" If, as has often been thought, this cry represents the struggle of the Christian who is *simul iustus et peccator* ("at the same time justified and sinner"), this would be a profound instance of Christian lament. Yet perhaps the majority of commentators now would hold the view that this cry gives voice to the pre-Christian experience of one still under the sway of "the law of sin and death" (Rom. 7:23, 25).[21] Even so, we might say that Paul recognizes a proper lamenting on behalf of the one who has not yet embraced the liberating power of Christ through the Spirit.

If we exclude Romans 7 from our purview, then the first demonstrable instance of lament in Romans actually involves the created order as a whole and not just human beings: "We know that the whole creation has been groaning as in the pains of childbirth right up to the present time" (8:22). As Laurie Braaten points out, the root Paul uses here for "groaning" (στενάζω) is regularly employed in the context of mourning and lamentation. Especially pertinent are those instances where the land "groans" (e.g., Isa. 21; Jer. 4:31) as the result of divine judgment, stemming from human iniquity.[22] Braaten makes a convincing case that the groaning of the earth in Romans 8 likewise follows from ongoing human sin and subsequent divine recompense, as opposed to a once-for-all "fall" of creation in the early chapters of Genesis. Human beings likewise "groan inwardly as we wait eagerly for our adoption to sonship, the redemption of our bodies" (8:23). The gap between present suffering and future deliverance could not be more evident, and Paul embraces the "groaning" that accompanies this expectation.

Romans 8:36, meanwhile, explicitly cites the lament from Psalm 44:22, "As it is written: "For your sake we face death all day long; we are considered as sheep to be slaughtered." Psalm 44 is a bona fide lament psalm, and we may cite the conclusion (vv. 25–26) as representative, "We are brought down to the dust; our bodies cling to the ground. Rise up and help us; rescue us because of your unfailing love." Paul for his part draws on the lament theme as a way of addressing the woes he endures for the gospel: "trouble . . . hardship . . . persecution . . . famine . . . nakedness . . . danger . . . sword . . ." While his lament is characteristically balanced with words of ultimate triumph (cf. the very next verse, "in all these things we are more than conquerors through him who loved us"), there is no question that Paul here draws directly on the lament tradition to make sense of his difficult life circumstances.[23]

If one is still tempted to argue that Paul's sense of ultimate conquering must necessarily cancel out any genuine anguish in his outlook, we need only counter with the paragraph in Romans 9 that follows Paul's citation of Psalm 44: "I speak the truth in

Christ—I am not lying, my conscience confirms it through the Holy Spirit—I have great sorrow and unceasing anguish in my heart" (Rom. 9:1–2). Though Paul's topic has changed, these verses demonstrate that an attitude of hope could coexist with sincere and deeply felt sorrow. It is notable that his discussion of Israel in chapters 9–11 includes two more items from the psalms: the hopeful notion from Psalm 94:4 that "God has not rejected his people" (Rom. 11:2), along with the more pessimistic assessment of the situation from Psalm 69:22–3: "May their table become a snare and a trap, a stumbling block and a retribution for them. May their eyes be darkened so they cannot see, and their backs be bent forever" (Rom. 11:9–10). If we may leave the Psalter for a moment, Paul expresses his distress at his countrymen's unbelief most powerfully in chapter 11 by invoking the reaction of the prophet Elijah: "Lord, they have killed your prophets and torn down your altars; I am the only one left, and they are trying to kill me" (Rom. 11:3, from 1 Kings 19:10, 14). Elijah's lament becomes Paul's own.

We may conclude this brief survey of Romans with an express call to lament: "mourn with those who mourn" (12:15). The statement is all the more noteworthy because the immediately preceding command is to "rejoice with those who rejoice." If continual joy were the necessary state of the true Christian (as one might infer from a hasty reading of Philippians 4:4 and similar passages), Paul ought to have stopped mid-verse. But he recognizes that people in the church do in fact grieve and that Christian love requires participation in our neighbors' sorrows.

Paul's penchant for lament in Romans is hardly an aberration across the corpus. Consider his prison soliloquy in Philippians: "If I am to go on living in the body, this will mean fruitful labor for me. Yet what shall I choose? I do not know! I am torn between the two: I desire to depart and be with Christ, which is better by far; but it is more necessary for you that I remain in the body" (Phil. 2:1:22–24). At one level, Paul rehearses his inner thoughts as a model of Christ-like service for the Philippians to emulate: just as Christ forsook heavenly glory for earthly service (2:5–11), so Paul prefers to aid the Philippians on earth rather than seek celestial joy with Jesus.[24]

But it is hard to square a perpetually happy, triumphalist Paul with the man here who in some sense would prefer death to his current circumstances. Recall, too, that Epaphroditus's healing was as much a mercy for Paul himself as it was for his friend: "But God had mercy on him, and not on him only but also on me, to spare me sorrow upon sorrow." Paul clearly had much sorrow in his life, and Epaphroditus's death would have been one blow too many.

Arguably, the height of Paul's theology and practice of lament lies in 2 Corinthians 4. The Corinthians were prone to criticize Paul for his path of suffering, under the assumption that a genuine messenger of God would be spared such indignities. Paul seeks to cut this assumption off at the knees and demonstrate that the way of suffering is the way of Jesus Christ, such that his suffering is the very seal of his apostleship. His words of lament in 2 Corinthians 4:7–12 are a crucial part of his argument:

> But we have this treasure in jars of clay to show that this all-surpassing power is from God and not from us. We are hard pressed on every side, but not crushed; perplexed, but not in despair; persecuted, but not abandoned; struck down, but not destroyed. We always carry around in our body the death of Jesus, so that the life of Jesus may also be revealed in our body. For we who are alive are always being given over to death for Jesus' sake, so that his life may also be revealed in our mortal body. So then, death is at work in us, but life is at work in you.

Through this series of paradoxical pairings, Paul speaks to the tension that lies at the heart of his Christian existence. It is not simply the case that he suffers for a while, but he also consoles himself with the truth that one day it will end. Nor, as we have seen, does the certainty of his now-and-not-yet victory cancel out his present experience of suffering. Rather, suffering and hope, grief and joy, somehow sit side by side in his soul. If this is the case, then his worship practice would presumably be defined by a similarly paradoxical blend of praise and lament. We get glimpses of precisely this blend in the examples of lament we have cited in the paragraphs above.

## *The Apostle James*

We have already noted James's recognition of the essential role of trials in the Christian life. Yet we must concede that he introduces trials with the advice to "count them all joy." One might conclude that James desires that people always maintain a cheerful countenance. In some situations, however, James offers very different counsel. To the divisive and quarrelsome, he writes, "Grieve, mourn and wail. Change your laughter to mourning and your joy to gloom. Humble yourselves before the Lord, and he will lift you up" (4:9–10). The lament here is clearly not a sorrow in the face of suffering, but rather a lament for one's own spiritual and moral bankruptcy.[25]

James also testifies to the fact that the cry for justice—a common feature of Old Testament lament—was still viable for the church. As a part of his excoriation of the unjust rich he declares, "Look! The wages you failed to pay the workers who mowed your fields are crying out against you. The cries of the harvesters have reached the ears of the Lord Almighty" (5:4). This lament echoes the words of Psalm 18 in its evocation of a cry "reaching the ears" of the Lord.[26] James may indeed exhort his people to patient endurance (cf. 1:2; 5:7), but this does not preclude the call for divine justice to be done in the face of oppression.

## *The Book of Revelation*

In Revelation 6:10, the cry for justice appears in pristine lament form in the question of the martyrs under the altar: "How long, Sovereign Lord, holy and true, until you judge the inhabitants of the earth and avenge our blood?"[27] The question springs from texts such as Psalm 6:3 (ESV), "My soul is also greatly troubled. But you, O Lord—how long?" and Psalm 13:1–2:

> How long, Lord? Will you forget me forever?
>   How long will you hide your face from me?
> How long must I wrestle with my thoughts
>   and day after day have sorrow in my heart?
> How long will my enemy triumph over me?

It is easy to lose track of this vignette from the fifth seal amid the many spectacular catastrophes of the apocalypse. Yet for all its brevity, this scene arguably sits near the pastoral heart of John's message. It addresses head-on questions that would have pressed on the minds of John's audience: Is it actually worth it to stand against the might of imperial Rome? Will the tangible benefits of compromise with the idolatrous world outweigh the mere promises of future bliss offered by the gospel? Is the church's life an unending series of torments at the hands of their oppressors?

John has an answer to each of these questions; but by playing his message out in dramatic narrative form, he enables his people's understandable fears to be addressed rather than sidestepped. The martyrs' cry acknowledges the difficulties of holding up under the daily pressure of life in the Roman Empire, such that the words of consolation at the close of the book are hard-won. John never takes the easy path of cheap assurance. Even here in chapter 6, while the martyrs receive a white robe as a symbol of their beloved status, they are told only that they should be patient "until the full number of their fellow servants, their brothers and sisters, were killed just as they had been." There will be ample opportunity for further lament on the part of the church before Jesus sets all things to right.

The specific call for vengeance here requires comment. Is *this* aspect of lament still valid for followers of the Prince of Peace who commands that we love our enemies? In response, we might first point out that the verb for "avenge" (ἐκδικέω) here is both lexically and contextually connected to divine *justice* rather than mere tit-for-tat bloodletting. This is not a question of taking matters into their own hands, but requesting that God uphold his righteous character. (Recall that Paul himself forbade his people from seeking retribution on their own, but followed that immediately with the exhortation, "leave room for God's wrath, for it is written: 'It is mine to avenge; I will repay,' says the Lord.") Moreover, the "souls" who call for this justice are in the presence of God and thus may be presumed to have a clear vision of the legitimacy of their case. They are meant to be understood as different from earthly vengeance seekers, who might be blind to their own transgressions and all too quick to heap up suffering upon others. Most critically, the severe persecution faced by John and his flock in the province of Asia puts them much more in the position of James's oppressed laborers than armchair theologians over coffee mooting the merits of non-retaliation. The ferocity of their oppressors triggers an equally strident call for divine retribution.

The lament of the saints in chapter 6 has an extended counterpart in the laments offered over Babylon in chapter 18. The book of Revelation regularly employs ironic reversal in its depiction of judgment upon the wicked (the most vivid example being 16:5: "You are just in these judgments, O Holy One, you who are and who were; for they have shed the blood of your holy people and your prophets, and you have given them blood to drink as they deserve."[28]) The fall of Babylon represents the answer to the prayer of the martyrs in 6:10, replete with the assurance that "he has avenged on her the blood of his servants." It is appropriate, then, that this fall includes tableaux of merchants and sea captains lamenting the demise of their beloved trading partner:

> "Woe! Woe to you, great city,
>   dressed in fine linen, purple and scarlet,
>   and glittering with gold, precious stones and pearls!
> In one hour such great wealth has been brought to ruin!" (18:16–17)

> "Woe! Woe to you, great city,
>   where all who had ships on the sea
>   became rich through her wealth!
> In one hour she has been brought to ruin!" (18:19)

A lament over the ruin of a desperately wicked city is, of course, not the final word in Revelation. The saints look forward to the day when the one seated on the throne will declare:

> Look! God's dwelling place is now among the people, and he will dwell with them. They will be his people, and God himself will be with them and be their God. "He will wipe every tear from their eyes.

There will be no more death or mourning or crying or pain, for the old order of things has passed away." (21:3–4)

Hope has the final word.

# Conclusion

It is true that the resurrection of Christ and his sending of the Spirit to the church means that the dominant note in New Testament texts is confidence and praise. But this stance of praise itself stands in paradoxical relationship with persistent suffering in present. The woes of this life are regularly acknowledged in the New Testament. Grief is not brushed under the rug but is instead acknowledged, often with the assistance of the Old Testament lament tradition. Jesus himself openly brings his troubles to God, and the apostles follow in his wake.

What changes, then, is not so much the sum total of lament, the absolute quantity of grief, but rather the circumstances in which that grief is experienced. The definitive act of God in Christ, most notably in his resurrection, casts its light upon even our darkest moments and offers hope for the future. By paying attention to the story of Jesus, we are enabled to burst the bonds of despair and gain perspective on the hope that awaits the faithful. We are indeed hard-pressed, perplexed, persecuted, and even struck down. Lament is therefore the proper response to such doleful circumstances. But our union with the risen Christ puts that lament into a context of ultimate deliverance:

> Therefore we do not lose heart. Though outwardly we are wasting away, yet inwardly we are being renewed day by day. For our light and momentary troubles are achieving for us an eternal glory that far outweighs them all. (2 Cor. 4:16–17)

# 5

# GOD THE TRINITY AND CHRISTIAN CARE FOR THOSE WHO LAMENT

Scott Harrower

**Introduction**

Discovering God and the ways in which he cares for us is critical for the art of discipleship. When we explore this, we find that God's unique Trinitarian nature and his presence in the Christian community enable him to care for Christians in deep and relevant ways, especially in the context and aftermath of trauma. In this chapter, I want to show that because God is *God the Trinity* he can work in empathetic, specific, and person-appropriate ways to aid our recovery from horrific events. Understanding what God's nature means for his care of others provides those who lament with the confidence that God is with them, working in visible and invisible ways to aid their recovery. God's presence and nature are important to consider because, if those who lament doubt these, they may easily fall into despair and spiritual apathy. So, part of the "good news" of the gospel is that when we suffer, we have God with us and he is working within all lamentable situations to care for us in attentive and specific ways.[1]

In what follows, I begin with lament—the valid and common experience of calling out to God in the midst of pain. I then reflect on 2 Corinthians and demonstrate that Christian lament occurs in the context of two communions: one divine and one ecclesial, Trinitarian and churchly contexts. We need to keep this big picture in mind. God's care in the context of lament involves him in shaping and guiding persons, as well as historical processes, in light of the resurrection of God the Son and the gift of the Spirit. A strong grip on these realities is necessary in order to perceive God's direct and indirect, visible and invisible, ways and instruments for caring for traumatized believers who lament. Recognizing these has profound practical implications for how we relate to God and to one another on the road to recovery from regrettable trauma.

## The Uniqueness of Christian Lament

When we suffer, we lament. But is this an appropriate response to suffering? Yes, it is, and 2 Corinthians demonstrates the validity as well as the uniqueness of *Christian lament*. The evidence for Christian lament in 2 Corinthians stems from glimpses into Paul's interrelated theological, mental, and emotional states in the wake of trauma. Paul himself did lament, and we have at least three references to some of these laments in 2 Corinthians. In order to make the case for the concrete historical reality of these early Christian laments, I identify them and note possible connections between these laments and a number of Paul's traumatic experiences. This is an important topic: I describe the connection between lament and trauma, because this is a physical and psychological reality that disturbs many of us today, and it also affects and scars those for whom we care. In addition, by acknowledging the reality of trauma as it relates to those who lament, we begin to appreciate the depths of what may be required of God and his church in order to renew and restore important aspects of the post-trauma lives of individuals and communities. That is, understanding the depths of healing required raises important questions of *what kind of care may be expected of God the Trinity by us, and what instruments of care he might be employ.* The systematic question at hand is: What is the relationship between "who" God is, "what" may he achieve, and "how" might he enable recovery from trauma and lament? The ecclesiological question is: How can we be available and involved in this important work? So, to start with, what is it about the Trinitarian nature of

God that enables him to establish person-specific and communally mediated foundations for recovering from trauma? Is there a clear connection between God's nature and his work to establish what is required for recovery from trauma—namely, a sense of safety, a coherent self-understanding, and reconnection to the community?

For the sake of clear understanding, allow me to offer a summary before outlining its components in the body of this chapter. In a nutshell, for Paul, God the Son's incarnation means that God has general empathy for all people who live in a world full of sin, suffering, lament, and trauma. Beyond this, God the Spirit's indwelling within each Christian allows a deeper and person-specific empathy for those who lament. Because God is One, God's general and specific empathy for his people is shared by the Father, Son, and Spirit. In light of this shared Trinitarian knowledge, we will see that God's Spirit in turn shares his concerns for a given individual believer with other members of the Christian community whom he also indwells. When God's empathetic and person-specific knowledge is shared across people, one person whom he indwells may receive specific insights about and gifts of care for another individual or community that is suffering and lamenting. In addition, God may support and strengthen these pastoral efforts by developing an attitude of service and gifted competence in the lives of those who minister alongside those who lament. Optimally, the cumulative outcome of these divine insights, motivations to care, and specific modes of care is that lamenters may be surrounded by God's support and healed to the point that not only do they honor and thank God, as well as his servants for their thoughtful care, but they may also be open to the possibility of sensitively cooperating in God's wider care for other people.

## Laments in 2 Corinthians

If we are going to say something sensible about the theological contours and pastoral implications of laments in the New Testament for Christians today, we need to identify and describe laments in the New Testament. Paul's second letter to the Corinthians provides a good example of his laments, because of his dire experiences leading up to the letter as well as the circumstances in which he wrote them. For these reasons that relate to suffering-oriented provenance, I will explore laments in 2 Corinthians.

## *Criteria for Identifying Laments in 2 Corinthians*

So, what do we mean when we say "lament"? Old Testament scholar Nathaniel Carlson perceptively writes that in the Old Testament "lament is the language of trauma."[2] Carlson provides a refreshingly succinct and insightful definition of biblical laments, such as those found in the psalms: these are *"expressions of painful emotion* (groaning, restlessness, terror, grief) against a backdrop of *traumatic experience* (mockery, ruin, destruction, violent assault, slaughter)."[3] From a New Testament perspective, Keith Campbell writes that a lament is a "distressful complaint/question/appeal directed toward God (a prayer) in order to work change for a real or perceived problem."[4] Campbell draws together a number of criteria for "delineating laments in the NT."[5] For Campbell, a New Testament lament is referred to or by a biblical author when at least one of the following is identified: (1) references to first-person, past laments, (2) select records of only a line from an actual lament; (3) allusions to Old Testament laments; (4) occasions where the mood of lament is appropriate and dominant; and (5) a full record of a lament prayer.[6]

Consistent with Campbell's criteria, Andrew Hassler finds laments in 2 Corinthians 1:8–11, 5:1–5, and 12:7–10.[7] He does so by finding "patterns of lament," rather than the Old Testament's "formal" kinds of laments.[8] For him, three criteria point out laments in Paul's letters.[9] To start with, the "fundamental elements of a lament" are "a severity of affliction, a petitioner crying out or groaning for deliverance, and a God who hears and promises to deliver, even while he may delay in acting."[10] Hassler concludes that in 2 Corinthians the markers of lament are mostly the "references" type, in which a personal lament is referred to but its precise content is not revealed.[11] He concludes that in each lament of 2 Corinthians

(1:8–11; 5:1–5; 12:7–10), the text refers to an occasion of lament by way of suggesting (1) a severe affliction, (2) supplication for deliverance, and (3) a certain kind of God (a personally engaged, powerful and responsive one).[12]

In this chapter, I will limit myself to the first of these laments in 2 Corinthians 1:8–11 (CSB).[13] The text reads:

> We don't want you to be unaware, brothers and sisters, of our affliction that took place in Asia. We were completely overwhelmed—beyond our strength—so that we even despaired of life itself. Indeed, we felt that we had received the sentence of death, so that we would not trust in ourselves but in God who raises the dead. He has delivered us from such a terrible death and he will deliver us. We have put our hope in him that he will deliver us again, while you join in helping us by your prayers. Then many will give thanks on our behalf for the gift that came to us through the prayers of many.

Because its content and sentiment are informed by the other laments, it is worth keeping 2 Corinthians 5:1–5 in mind:

> For we know that if our earthly tent we live in is destroyed, we have a building from God, an eternal dwelling in the heavens, not made with hands. Indeed, we groan in this tent, desiring to put on our heavenly dwelling, since when we have taken it off, we will not be found naked. Indeed, we groan while we are in this tent, burdened as we are, because we do not want to be unclothed but clothed, so that mortality may be swallowed up by life. Now the one who prepared us for this very purpose is God, who gave us the Spirit as a down payment.

What is important for our purposes here is that an exploration of 2 Corinthians 1:8–11 reveals that Paul's experience and theology of lament operates in a Trinitarian and ecclesial context.

## *Lament in the Context of Impending Death*

This passage refers to Paul's laments during some particularly traumatic times. Though it does not detail the lament itself, it refers the reader to Paul's previous experiences of lament and therefore meets Hassler's first criterion for counting as a record of a lament.

In this portion of 2 Corinthians, Paul states that his experiences were generated by a series of events in Asia. He writes that he and his companions "were so utterly burdened beyond our strength that we despaired for life itself" (1:8b). Paul (and Timothy, since both men sent the letter) emphasizes the severity of this experience by immediately restating it as "We felt that we had received the sentence of death" (1:9a). Following the lead of Harris, I take the expectation of "death" as referring to the apparent inevitability of dying physically. This is Paul's way of saying he believed that death would be the immediate consequence of a number of life-threatening situations he experienced—shipwrecks, prolonged tortures and their aftereffects, as well as mob assaults.[14] Paul vividly describes the psychology these afflictions involved:

> We are afflicted in every way but not crushed; we are perplexed, but not driven to despair; we are persecuted, but not abandoned; we are struck down, but not destroyed. We always carry the death of Jesus in our body. (2 Cor. 4: 8–10)

In addition, in 2 Corinthians 11:23–32, he relates an anthology of suffering and trauma that sheds light on the way in which these were experienced, including "imprisonments, far worse beatings, many times near death" (11:23). He also gives precise and personal definitions: "Five times I received the forty lashes minus one. . . . Three times I was beaten with rods. Once I received a stoning. Three times I was shipwrecked. I have spent a night and a day in the open sea" (11:24–25). Paul also experienced great fear, and he felt threatened by impending suffering. Verse 26 repeats the word *danger* in order to emphasize this:

> On frequent journeys, I faced dangers from rivers, dangers from robbers, dangers from my own people, dangers from Gentiles, dangers in the city, dangers in the wilderness, dangers at sea, and dangers among false brothers.

The persistence of these dangers stands out in "toil and hardship, many sleepless nights, hunger and thirst, often without food, cold and without clothing. Not to mention other things, there is the daily pressure on me: my concern for all the churches" (11:27–28).

Many of Paul's experiences, especially in the context of believing that he was doomed to die, can be medically and psychologically described as trauma. According to the American Psychiatric Association's DSM-5, trauma is "exposure to actual or threatened death, serious injury, or sexual violence."[15] Trauma is "any serious event that threatens or affects the life or physical integrity of a person, or a loved one. Experiencing, witnessing, or becoming aware of such an event creates intense fear, helplessness, or horror in the affected person."[16] According to the APA, Paul's experiences of overwhelming dangerous and violent situations suggest that he experienced trauma.

The consequences of trauma are profound and lasting. Trauma "so overwhelms the capacities of victims to take it in, that the violence cannot be absorbed as it is happening. Traumatic violence comes as a shocking blow, a terrifying disruption of normal mental processes, distorting reality, even as it becomes the only reality."[17] Because trauma is overwhelming and distorts perceptions of reality, Shelly Rambo describes it as haunting and ubiquitous:

> "*After the storm*" is always here. . . . It is an event that continues, that persists in the present. Trauma is what does not go away. It persists in symptoms that live on in the body, in the intrusive fragments of memories that return. It persists in symptoms that live on in communities, in the layers of past violence that constitute present ways of relating. . . . Life after the storm, people in New Orleans can tell you, is not life as they once knew it. It is life continually marked by ongoing death.[18]

Given the gravity of trauma and its aftereffects, Rambo and other authors in the field of trauma studies ask, "How do people, whose hearts and minds have been wounded by violence, come to feel and know the redeeming power of God's grace?"[19] How did Paul cope with his traumas? A primary way is to cry out to God—and the kind of God to whom he cried out is vital to the crying out itself.

## Crying out to God

A number of features of 2 Corinthians 1:9 and 1:10 suggest that in the midst of this experience, Paul and his companions would have cried out to God in distress and asked for rescue. These include the confident comment that "he [God] has delivered us from such a terrible death" (1:10). Second, the result of crying out to God results in a personally verified (hence warranted) knowledge of God's power (1:9b). Third, this knowledge confirms the belief that prayer is powerful to bring about "help"—presumably favorable changes in deathly circumstances (1:11).

Other attestations to Paul's lament-like pleas to God in the context of distress support the view that such crying out to God for help is an appropriate Christian response to danger. Acts 27 has much to say about Paul's ongoing experiences of God, as well as his confidence in the divine knowledge of his plight and the prospect of rescue, despite the threat of death in a shipwrecking storm. In that story, Paul's words and practices are consistent with both crying out to God and his confidence of divine aid despite imminent death. For example, in the midst of the storm, Paul uses the ritual of the Eucharist to rehearse his confidence in God based on past deliverance: he acts out Jesus' pattern of praying, breaking bread, and sharing it. God then speaks and mediates a message of survival through Paul that there will be life after the storm (Acts 27:13–44).

We know that Paul cried out to God, but what was Paul expecting when he cried out to God in the midst of being emotionally and physically battered? What was it about God that gave him the confidence to plead for practical aid and change in circumstance? What could a heavenly, immaterial, and spiritual being such as God possibly do for an individual who laments here in the world below? Answers to these questions are partly provided by noting the Trinitarian substance and contours of Paul's thought. This can strengthen our perspective on whether we can trust God to know our plight, and it also helps us structure our expectations and hope for how God may involve us in his work of comforting and restoring those Christians who lament.

## Trinitarian Empathy for Christians Who Lament

Though few people would claim that God is apathetic about his people's suffering, some Christians in the context of trauma and lament could reasonably ask how it is possible for God to understand what the experiences of trauma and lament are like *for human beings*. More precisely, how does he knowingly understand what the experiences of trauma and lament are like for them? Further, how could God know how to bring the best appropriate help and healing in each individual situation? In other words, how can God care for us thoughtfully and personally when we lament? God's empathy for people is the foundation for how he may know our plight and relevantly care for us. His exceptional ability to empathize with each believer is enabled by his distinctive Trinitarian nature and actions in history.[20]

## Human Empathy for Those Who Lament

Since humans are created in the image of God, we have specific kinds of knowledge available to us, which includes empathy. This unique human ability entails a form of "mind reading" in which one person can understand the mental/emotional states of other people as if these were their own experience.[21] Eleonore Stump writes that, because we have mirror neurons in our brains, we are capable of a limited form of mind-reading and hence empathy for a person in our presence: "In mind-reading, one person knows intuitively something about what another person is doing and with what motive and emotion he is doing it."[22] So empathy is a special kind of knowledge of other persons who are near us, which is gained by the mode of mirror neurons; it cannot be gained remotely from those for whom we might have empathy.

It is important to point out that genuine empathy is not self-serving; it is not an end in itself. Rather, it enables an other-person centeredness—that is, a deep and real openness to another person. Empathy requires and entails an openness in which one's emotional life is offered in empathetic service to another: "Empathy is not a desire to alleviate the suffering of others; it is an orientation toward others' emotions that makes these emotions salient and enables others' distress to get a grip on us, to matter or to count."[23] Empathy therefore results in "psychic integration" between people, which allows for closeness rather than distance between them, even in the often isolating circumstances of lament.[24] This raises the theological question of how God has empathy for us humans. If he is a spirit and thus lacks motor neurons, can he be empathetically engaged with human beings?

### *General Empathy for People: The Incarnation*

God has profound empathy for human beings because God the Son added a human nature to himself. Paul promotes divine empathy via the incarnation in 2 Corinthians, which is the same Epistle in which he mentioned his extreme trauma and lament. Sure, the incarnation of God the Son is a profound theological resource across Paul's theology (see Phil. 2:6–11), but it is interesting to note that he deploys it for pastoral ends in 2 Corinthians 8:9: "For you know the grace of our Lord Jesus Christ: Though he was rich, for your sake he became poor, so that by his poverty you might become rich."

By taking on a human nature, God the Son experiences "poverty"; God the Son experiences human suffering and lament from a first-person perspective.[25] God the Son incarnate has an insider's perspective on human suffering and lament within the limitations, frustrations, and travails of common human beings.[26] Therefore, he understands what *you* may go through in suffering. The book of Hebrews tells us that in his incarnate state, God the Son suffered, cried, and groaned to God as he learned the pain and difficulty of obedience in the context of testing and many trials (Heb. 5:7–8); in this way, he can empathize with human frailty and affliction (Heb. 4:15). This knowledge is shared across the hypostatic union so that we can say without doubt that God has this mode and content of knowledge. Therefore, God the Trinity perceives suffering from the insider's perspective consistent with

God the Son's incarnation. Thus God genuinely can appreciate generally known truths from a lived-in human perspective, because Jesus experienced tiredness, hunger, harassment, discrimination, grief, and thirst; and this generates empathy, because Jesus has the neurological mirror system that gives him the capacity to know and perceive the general experiences of the suffering of other human beings to some degree. In light of this, we can refer to God the Son's incarnation-based empathy as a "general empathy" for human beings. By extension from "general empathy," and in the light of his own suffering, God the Son can knowingly say, "I have experienced human lament." It is important to note that Jesus' experiences and empathy inform his shepherding, his care for his people. His general empathy is the precursor to bringing about change and relief for other persons; it entails shepherding and guiding people through, away from, and in the aftermath of harm. It means understanding, protecting, and guiding people who are harassed. God's empathy means that God has an insider's insight into the fact that he needs to offer refreshment for the fatigued and encouragement as well as help for those tempted to give up or give in to temptation.

*Particular Empathy: The Indwelling of the Spirit*

God is with us; we never suffer alone. And because God is *in* us, we can also have the hope that he has a particular empathy for each individual Christian in addition to his general empathy for us. Early on in 2 Corinthians, Paul writes that God "has also put his seal on us and given us the Spirit in our hearts as a down payment" (1:22). This is the same Spirit who "searches the depths" of God and people, and who knows the wisdom of God with respect to both God and people (1 Cor. 2:10). This means that God is with and in us, as the God who knows what is really going on and how it feels to be in our situation. God knows people in an exceptional, internal, empathetic mode and to a matchless degree when he indwells them. Because God the Spirit indwells a person (which extends to God the Trinity), God has a unique mode of knowledge and perspective from which he knows that person. He has an inner-personal (internal to the believer) mode of knowledge into people because his life is joined to theirs, so he knows their life in tandem with his union with them. Therefore, as a result of indwelling people, God understands the particularities of personal experience "from the inside" and also in line with the good and ultimate direction in which he is orienting their life. God accesses their mental and emotional perception of the world "hand in hand," as it were. He can empathize with them in any given situation because he is in them and united to them, so he is necessarily involved within the structure of their being and the cooperative supernatural direction of their life. I refer to this kind of empathy as "person-specific" or "person-particular" empathy.

The particular mode of empathy that the Spirit may have for a person is coordinated and consistent with the general empathy that God the Son has due to his incarnation. We can then add to this the unity of God's consciousness that guarantees that the entire Godhead empathizes with each believer both generally and specifically. Importantly, the unity of God's life means that any divine actions resulting from God's empathy are willed and coordinated without conflict between the Father, Son, and Holy Spirit.

## Shared Attention, Emotion, and Focus within the Godhead

God does much more than merely know about our lamentable lives. God knows, God cares—and God acts. Because people are collectively and individually his image, he often acts through us to care for one another in the context of lament. But how does God share his knowledge with people?

Shared attention occurs when two persons understand each other and each other's state of mind to the point where they can mutually focus on something at the same time together. In addition, they are able to understand that in so doing they are participating in a shared experience with the other person, with the result that what is experienced is profoundly shaped by it being co-experienced. The capacity for shared attention is a foundational mental and relational capacity for personal beings. As Marion Hourdequin writes, "Shared intentionality . . . involves responding to and sharing others' emotions, identifying the objects of others' attention, discerning and sharing others' goals, cooperative communication, and coordinated social interaction."[27] Shared attention may flow on to shared intentions and actions.

It should go without saying that, within the unity of God's oneness, all knowledge is shared between the Father, Son, and Spirit. In tandem with this, all of God's intentions are willed by God's single divine will. There is nothing the Spirit knows that the Father and the Son do not know, and as a result God's empathetic response is the response of the whole Godhead. This absolute unity of knowledge, empathetic concern, and actions toward people is possible among the persons of the Godhead because God is a single, simple, immaterial being whose persons have their life in one another.[28] The "psychological analogy" for the life of the Trinity is a historic analogy that helps us understand the possibility of the unity of divine life, willing, and action. This highlights the important point that God's spiritual life is the foundation for his shared attention, intentions, and actions.[29] This metaphysical unity guarantees that there will never be a miscommunication or misfiring within God's shared empathy, shared attention, shared intentions, or shared actions. While such a nonfragmented interpersonal closeness and shareability is not possible in relationships between human persons, it does occur uniquely and without impediment within God.[30]

*There are profound pastoral outcomes of divine shared attention, empathy, and intentionality, because God's united knowledge and concern can be shared with his images for the sake of carrying out his well-informed and caring intentions.* Because of God's presence in individual believers and in the church by the Spirit of the Son, *God shares his attention, empathy, and intentions with some people for the sake of caring appropriately and specifically for others.*

## God Shares His Attention, Empathy, and Intention with His Images

How can we be involved in God's care for people in the midst and aftermath of trauma and lament? A vital part of this trades on the fact that God shares his insights and intentions with people who are united to him in Christ and by the Spirit. Because of union with Christ, Christians experience a wholesale reformulation of their perspective on the world—and this includes our perspective on those who experience trauma and lament. Paul writes that he no longer regards Christ or any person from a merely human point of view; rather, the mind of God and the love of God provide a renovated vantage point from which to perceive persons (1 Cor. 2:16). Hence, people who are being renewed into images of Christ have Christ's own perspective: "We do not know anyone from a worldly perspective" (2 Cor. 5:16). For this reason, Paul continues, "Therefore, if anyone is in Christ, he is a new creation; the old has passed away, and see, the new has come! Everything is from God" (5:17–18a). Images of God may become images of Christ. As part of this transformation, they receive various degrees of God's perspective on people and history, and they may more deeply understand and mediate God's message to others on his behalf: "We are ambassadors for Christ, since God is making his appeal through us: Be reconciled to God" (5:20). God's frame of reference is shared with believers by the Spirit, who is Lord. This vantage point is oriented toward reconciliation with God; therefore, it makes sense that the mind, heart, and soul of a person should also be reconciled to God's point of view (2 Cor. 5). For these reasons, Paul can say that Jesus has shared his attention and intentions with Paul: "We have known the mind of Christ" (1 Cor. 2:16).

God also draws people into his concerns for individuals and groups, including those who lament. Because God is the one who said "Let light shine out of darkness" and has "shone in our hearts to give the light of the knowledge of God's glory in the face of Jesus Christ" (2 Cor. 4:6), he can overcome the default of human selfishness and generate a caring perspective in believers. This leads to empathy, and there is a profound example of this in 2 Corinthians where we see that God generates empathy within Paul for the Corinthians. So God knows Paul's concern for the Corinthians and, to help Paul in his mission to help the Corinthians, God shares with Titus some of Paul's empathy. In 2 Corinthians 8:16, Paul writes, "Thanks be to God who put the same concern for you into the heart of Titus." This shows us that God can actively draw believers, such as Titus, into what God and his disciples, such as Paul, know and care about with respect to the needs of others. This is an example of God enabling shared empathy between two individuals for a common cause.

We also have an example of God working for the good of people by means of sharing his concerns with a group of people. The Macedonian Christians exemplified this for Paul, in that "they gave themselves first to the Lord and then to us by God's will" (8:5). The Macedonians cared for Paul and his coworkers, as well as for impoverished Christians in Jerusalem, because "by God's will" they were motivated them to "give themselves" to others and pursue their good—which in this case, took the form of financial sharing. God actively drew this community into his concerns for people, and they responded appropriately. When the Macedonians perceived God's concerns, they met this through practical actions of joyful generosity (8:2). Such astounding actions result from a deep transformation that God himself brings about in individuals and communities.

## Transformation

When we lament, we often see ourselves as useless and stuck in both time and our sorry state. One of the powerful messages from 2 Corinthians is that, even though Paul and his companions suffered greatly, they were cared for by God and also used as instruments of God's care. In other words, being traumatized and "living after the storm" of trauma do not disqualify us from being renewed and included in God's care for his people. Even if we are those who have participated in, or directly committed, heinous evils such as

Paul himself had, we are not beyond God's progressive and transformative work. Spirit-empowered metamorphosis is available to all believers.[31]

Transformation means there can be discipleship in, through, and after trauma—whether we are the victims or the perpetrators. Whereas God knowing us is the basis of his empathy for us, our knowledge of him is the basis of our involvement in his good works. The believer's transformation begins with existentially and epistemologically perceiving Jesus for who he is, and then by extension understanding ourselves as those who need to receive grace in order to become like him: "We all, with unveiled faces, are looking as in a mirror at the glory of the Lord and are being transformed into the same image from glory to glory; this is from the Lord who is the Spirit" (3:18). Believers receive the freedom of a new perspective on Christ and the message and ministry that brings life and righteousness (3:1–9, 17). Hence, we have the responsibility to act righteously with respect to others, and this righteousness takes on a special importance when it comes to relating to lamenters, who have often been profoundly wounded. Relationships with those to whom God calls us to minister require the transformation of our desires and emotions, as well as our competency for ministering to others. This is a high calling, but not one we attempt on the basis of our own skills and ability.

## Competence for Care: The Power of the Son and Spirit for the Sake of Life

Some may refrain for caring for others on God's behalf because they fear they will make a mess of things. Once we have experienced trauma, we may be particularly hesitant to become involved in situations that involve pain. Others will be hesitant because they believe they may not be up to it—physically, or (more likely) emotionally or intellectually. At this point, Paul's reflections in the wake of his own traumatic experiences are important for us today. One way Paul encourages us is via the resurrection of Jesus from the dead. Notice that in the first of Paul's laments in 2 Corinthians—"God who raises the dead"—plays the role of giving Paul hope for the apparently impossible (1:9). Paul previously wrote to the Corinthians about the uniqueness of the Christian God as the one who alone "raises the dead."[32] Not only is the past resurrection of Jesus a pointer to what God can do, but it also points to what God is actively bringing about in the present to specifically care for those who lament.

The risen Christ is working to bring new life to his people by means of his Spirit-empowered disciples. Paul writes that Christ is the one who leads a "triumphal procession," yet it is "though us"— Paul and his companions—that he "spreads the aroma of the knowledge of him in every place" (2:14). This knowledge is the "aroma of life leading to life" (2:16). Paul immediately asks, "Who is adequate for these things?" He knows that this life-giving work among people is possible only by the power of the Spirit. The work of disciples and the Spirit converge together under Christ's Lordship. For this reason, Paul writes that the Corinthian believers are the work of God through Paul and his mission teams: the church is "Christ's letter, delivered by us, not written with ink but with the Spirit of the living God" (3:3). This competence is a life-giving kind of competence, as illustrated in 6:14–7:4. The power of God's ministry of life though the gifts given to the church (such as prophecy, apostleship, and so on) can even rescue and reform those who are currently lost to death.[33] The coordination between God the Spirit and life is also central to Paul's lament reference in 2 Corinthians 5:1–5.

## God Comforts People through One Another

A particular ecclesiology is reflected in Paul's praises. It is distinctively Christian because it is the net result of Paul's Trinitarianism and his emphasis on Christlikeness. He exclaims:

> Blessed be the God and Father of our Lord Jesus Christ, the Father of mercies and the God of all comfort. He comforts us in all our affliction, so that we may be able to comfort those who are in any kind of

affliction, through the comfort we ourselves receive from God. For just as the sufferings of Christ overflow to us, so also through Christ our comfort overflows. (2 Cor. 1:3–5)

As noted above, God can comfort people specifically because he knows them intimately and knows the situations over which they lament. In this passage, we see the intent of his comfort and once again the fact that he mediates his comfort through people. Like empathy, comfort is an end in itself: it always reaches out for the good of the other. This requires what Paul refers to as finding room for one another in our hearts (6:14–7:4).[34] By doing so, we reflect God's goodness and grace to one another; and for this reason, we can draw on Paul to say that an important point of comforting one another is helping each other see what Paul calls "the grace of God in you" (9:14). God is present and at work in lamenters, even after trauma. Because his grace is his immaterial, invisible presence, and power at work for the sake of life, *it is often not perceived by those who lament, so they need others to make it clear.* Since Paul knows that some of his recipients may not perceive God's kindness in their own lives, he asks rhetorically, "Do you yourselves not recognize that Jesus Christ is in you?" (13:5). However, the fact is that Paul has strong evidence for how this dynamic worked out in his life, as well as in the lives of Titus and the Macedonians.

## Conclusion: The Ecclesiological Question

In sum, when we lament we can plead with the God who has both general and specific empathy for us. God's interest in us and his active care are both good news for us. So, let's be open to being mediums of God's empathetic care for his children. This call is a vital aspect of our vocations as members of the Kingdom of God. Also, let's trust and be open to God's care when he sends Christlike people into our lives. I wonder what our prayer lives would look like if we were to offer ourselves to God as messengers of his care and recipients of his empathetic love.

In addition to these imperatives, we need to consider the corporate and ecclesial questions that arise out of a systematic consideration of the divine and human interpersonal relationships discussed above. For example: What kind of ecclesiology would support the empathetic work of God the Trinity? Or, rather, what kind of ecclesiology would be generated by the empathetic ministry of God through his people? The question readily comes to mind of what kind of ecclesiology is brought about by Trinitarian concern and action mediated through human beings. The flip side of this is to consider what kind of ecclesiology would support empathetic and attentive human relatedness that is grounded in the nature and works of God the Trinity. These questions, especially as they relate to the historic missions of God in the world, may be developed in future research. It would require developing and deploying the notion of "alongsidedness" and "accompaniment" in conversation with righteousness, responsibility, and gifts in the church. These ideas are reflections of realities that have already taken place: believers are already seated "alongside" one another as coheirs of the kingdom and as co-participants in the heavenly wedding banquet of Christ. We "accompany" one another as fellow pilgrims who are already on our way to the heavenly city. The Trinitarian, communal, and eucharistic aspects of this may be helpfully explored in in conversation with the works of Charles Cardinal Journet.[35] Among his relevant ideas is the claim that the church *is* a concrete mission of God's Spirit in the sense that the best moments of concern and care in the church are instances in which we most clearly see what God's Spirit is like.[36]

# 6

## "There Is a Balm in Gilead": A Call to Lament Together

### Emmett G. Price III

"Oh that my head were waters,
    and my eyes a fountain of tears,
that I might weep day and night
    for the slain of the daughter of my people!"[1]

Jeremiah 9:1


"Jesus wept."

John 11:35

During a recent trip to the Museum of African American History and Culture in Washington, D.C., I was tremendously distraught as I gazed upon the remnant of *São José Paquete d' Africa*.[2] In December 1794, this Portuguese slave ship set sail from the colony of Mozambique in southeast Africa for Maranhao, a slave port in the northeast corner of Brazil.[3] Four weeks into the journey, the vessel and its cargo—hundreds of stolen African progeny—sank near Cape Town, South Africa.[4] Two hundred years later, the iron ballast blocks used to weigh the ship down were discovered and retrieved by the divers of the Slave Wrecks Project and are now on exhibit at the museum.[5] Seemingly lifeless, the historic relics appeared suspended under a faint light in a dark, cold antechamber. Three levels below the ground, these iron ballast blocks serve as the sole narrators left to tell the story of "the slain of the daughter of my people."

Like Jesus, I wept. As I embraced the anger, frustration, sadness, and pain—while spontaneously and publicly mourning countless generations of "God's children" subjected to the most heinous torture at the hands of other humans—I heard the robust baritone of Paul Robeson singing "There Is a Balm in Gilead."[6] As I looked around to see if anyone else heard him, I realized that people from around the world—a variety of hues, ethnicities, and nationalities from numerous ancestries—were also weeping.

As I saw in that museum, the narrative of the transatlantic slave trade is a global tragedy. Although it is often told through the lens of the Black American experience, the narrative of the transatlantic slave trade embodies a story of human sin that is felt deep within when we allow ourselves to feel. In that moment I wondered, as I do now, why in that dimly lit, cold room with iron ballast blocks did we not all come together for a moment of communal lament?

In the foreword to Soong-Chan Rah's critical reading of Lamentations, *Prophetic Lament: A Call for Justice in Troubled Times*,[7] Brenda Salter McNeil offers her perspective on the challenge of communal lament:

> "The Church has lost its ability to lament!" This heartfelt cry came from a seminary student as she prayed with other graduate students, faculty and staff who gathered together to seek God for racial justice and reconciliation throughout our nation. As we cried and prayed together we realized that our theology and spiritual formation hadn't given us sufficient permission, language or tools to adequately sit with the despair and sadness of recent racial injustices, senseless acts of gun violence and social unrest taking place in the world around us. We even saw this on social media where people also seemed paralyzed and helpless to know what to do and how to respond. Sincere, well-meaning Christian people asked, "What should we do?" while people who were fed up with the seeming indifference of those around them expressed their outrage through a hashtag that proclaimed "Silence is violence!"[8]

The communal need for lament is inherent to the human condition. We will all, at some point and during some season in life, experience intense grief or sorrow stemming from external trauma enacted by another human or aggregation of humans. Human suffering at the hands of one another is a constant in the cycle of human history dating back to Cain's murder of his brother Abel (Gen. 4:1–18). Cain's treacherous decision to murder his brother had an impact not only on the two of them and their extended family but also on all humanity. It is this wider impact that calls for us to move from individual to communal lament. Yet, as with my experience as well as the one mentioned by McNeil, we are challenged in our ability to transition from the individual laments of our weeping prophet and our weeping Savior to communal lament as part of our liturgical praxis. This chapter aims to challenge the church of the twenty-first century to reimagine and reengage in the sacred practice of lament as a spiritual discipline—not merely as an individual transactional practice to assuage traumatic moments, but as one that displays our intentional love for each other.

## "There Is a Balm in Gilead, to Make the Wounded Whole"

Whether reading, singing, or praying the various biblical passages of lament, the depths of pain, suffering, agony, and in some cases defeat, resonate strongly and loudly. In one of Jeremiah's many laments, he is distraught because Zion is overthrown and Israel is in exile. In quite an expressive fashion and formulated as a creative work, Jeremiah's lament offers intense grief, uncontrollable tears, and brokenhearted displays of both empathy and sympathy.

> My eyes are spent with weeping;
> > my stomach churns;
> my bile is poured out to the ground
> > because of the destruction of the daughter of my people,
> because infants and babies faint
> > in the streets of the city. (Lam. 2:11)

God warned that destruction would come if disobedience ensued. While God's anger was revealed, God's compassion, mercy, and faithfulness were also equally on display. God's instructional invitation to Solomon in 2 Chronicles 7:11–22 was in effect for numerous generations at the time of the fall of Jerusalem in 586 BC. Although the wounds were not removed, God did avail a pathway toward healing.

Weeping and, more importantly, lamenting are gifts to the human condition because they force us to feel the depth and agony of sorrow in a manner that, although uncontrollable, has an end. Feeling and the intentional action of being present are essential to the process of lamenting. As we feel uncontrollable rage, we are reminded of the sovereignty of God—the God who created the heavens and the earth (Gen. 1:1). As we wrestle with our fears, we are reminded of the God who "gave us a spirit not of fear but of power and love and self-control" (2 Tim. 1:7). As we feel our brokenness, our heartache, and—even as Jeremiah expressed—the inability to control our bowels, we remember God as our creator, protector, defender, sustainer, and the supplier of our daily bread.[9] It is in our weakest state that we learn best how to trust in the One who is able to keep us from stumbling and present us blameless before the presence of his glory with great joy.[10]

John's Gospel narrative of the resurrection of Lazarus offers a perspective that is critical for the twenty-first-century church: God incarnate cares and feels our sorrows (see John 11:33–38). John reveals Jesus' ultimate intention of publicly glorifying God through the resurrection of Lazarus, both as a theological and an eschatological exercise. Although the grieving guests of Mary and Martha may have misinterpreted the dual nature of his being fully human and fully divine, it should not be lost on us that his fully human sentiment was the deep hurt and loss felt by all who were present. Jesus loved Lazarus, and he shared in the temporary state of sorrow, joining others in a communal lament. Jesus also knew, however, that the moment of lament would not be the conclusion to this complex experience. Here, Jesus teaches us how to mourn, even how to lament, with a gaze to the hope eternal. Jesus not only reveals hope, but he also stands as our hope. "Father, I thank you that you have heard me. I knew that you always hear me, but I said this on account of the people standing around, that they may believe that you sent me" (John 11:41–42). Jesus offers a unique glimpse of this eternal hope by raising Lazarus from the dead as a physical example of the divine, eschatological reality for all believers. In his divinity, Jesus raised Lazarus from the dead; in his humanity, Jesus lamented with Mary and the gathered mourners. He shows us that communal lament is not only necessary, it is biblical.

Jesus is the balm in our proverbial Gilead to make us, the wounded, whole. Jesus reminds us of the value and purpose of communal lament as exemplified in the psalms of lament. Within the Old Testament psalter are the poetic expressions of worship by and for the Hebrew children and their progeny. Beyond the variety of themes explored within the psalter, each of the five books contains calls to worship, benedictions, songs of praise, prayers, articulations of gratitude, and laments as regular modes of individual and collective dialogue with God. Psalms of lament are a critical mass within the one hundred and fifty divisions of the psalter. With fifty psalms including laments (both individual and communal), the Hebrew children and their offspring understood the importance and urgency of lament.

Within Jewish liturgical praxis, lament (both individual and communal) remains a fixture. In fact, even individual laments are used to catalyze communal lament. An example of this is found in David's Psalm 69, which is one of the most quoted within the New Testament. It simultaneously functions as David's personal expression of deep emotions, as well as a congregational song and communal prayer. The individual experience is intensified by the collective engagement in a process of not only remembrance but also a forewarning to not repeat. Psalm 69 offers David's dark, distressed, and depressed sentiments fueled by frustration, fear, and imminent danger. Here, he remarks that it is his unwavering faith and obedience to God that is causing his misfortune, which is dramatically different from Jeremiah's articulation. Yet his complaints are honest, vivid, and exhausting. He moves past his complaint to confess his sin, and then he continues to seek God's help. David moves on to curse his enemies before offering praise to God. His personal moment of distress, as articulated through this psalm of lament, emerges as a collective call for communal lament by and for the Jewish people. Jesus understood this as he joined Mary and the mourners on the fourth day after Lazarus was buried. God incarnate feels our pain, cares deeply for our sorrows, and offers us divine hope for tomorrow individually but also, and more importantly, together.

## "There Is a Balm in Gilead, to Heal the Sin-Sick Soul"

The church of Jesus Christ in the United States has continuously missed the opportunity to share together in communal lament. This ecumenical body of diverse believers has failed to lament the mass genocide of countless generations of indigenous people who inhabited and nurtured native lands before papal bulls provided a pathway toward colonization as a part of the Doctrine of Discovery.[11] This same church has failed to collectively lament the torture and generational trauma of the stolen daughters and sons of African soil. This multiethnic, multicultural aggregation of believers has failed to lament the subjugation of women and people of color to subordinate roles during the rise of democracy. The church of Jesus Christ in the United States has continuously failed to collectively lament with the people of Japan, Korea, and other nations decimated by war and inhumane treatment over multiple generations. Amid so many situations, scenarios, and seasons of sorrow where the church of the United States at large failed to join Jesus as he wept for his beloved, this church also failed to lament the horrendous lynching of fourteen-year-old Emmett Louis Till on August 28, 1955, in the Delta region of Mississippi.[12] Communal lament is still needed for the Jim Crow era animus and torment toward nonwhite citizens by an un-Christlike segment of God's children blinded by the sin of hatred. Communal lament in these and many other situations and seasons may certainly remind us all of the apostle Paul's call to unity through his admonition in Ephesians 4: "There is one body and one Spirit—just as you were called to the one hope that belongs to your call—one Lord, one faith, one baptism, one God and Father of all, who is over all and through all and in all" (Eph. 4:4–6). Our failure to gather together for communal lament has only led to further separation and segmentation, calling forth more tragedy, more division, and less hope.

Similar to the vicious murder of Emmett Louis Till (14), the equally tragic murders of Trayvon Benjamin Martin (17), Michael Brown Jr. (18), Jordan Davis (17), Hadiya Pendleton (15), Tamir Rice (12), Tony Terrell Robinson Jr. (19), William L. Chapman II (18), Laquan McDonald (17), and Paul O'Neal (18)—all teenagers of color—would have been the source of tears for Jeremiah and for Jesus. Yet the church as a whole remains unmoved and uninterested in gathering across our divided lines to lament the loss of our children. In essence, we refuse to "weep with those who weep" (Rom. 12:15).

Similar to the vocal outrage and calls for public prayer after the bombing of the 16th Street Baptist Church in Birmingham, Alabama, on September 15, 1963, by four members of the Ku Klux Klan, there were tepid and sparse calls for prayer and lament after the vicious murders of the nine prayer warriors at Emmanuel African American Methodist Episcopal Church in Charleston, South Carolina, on the evening of Wednesday, June 17, 2015.[13] Yet even then, the moment was too brief, the weeping was too short, and the collective outcry was too mild. Lament is an expression of worship. After any cataclysmic catastrophe, we must change the way we engage in worship. Worship is relational and transformative. Our worship engages God on God's terms reflective of God's character, nature, and sentiments. If God cares, feels our sorrow, and offers divine hope, then we should strive to do the same with and for one another.

In our current season, defined by hashtags and slogans referencing realized pain and trauma, our collective engagement with God must shift toward a greater awareness of what it means to be a part of the Christian body and what it means to worship in community. Communal worship that fails to acknowledge the pain, suffering, and trauma of some tends to do more harm to the whole. Classic questions, such as one asked by Don E. Saliers in *Worship Come to Its Senses*, aids in stimulating self-reflective and introspective assessment of our understanding of the responsibility of worshipping in "spirit and in truth" (John 4:24).[14] Saliers asks, "What makes Christian worship true and relevant, and how can our liturgical gatherings shape and express authentic Christian faith and life in the world of everyday?"[15] Similarly, in *Worship and the Reality of God: An Evangelical Theology of Real Presence*, John Jefferson Davis, after visiting thirty-five different congregations during a research sabbatical, asks, "Is there a vivid consciousness of the presence of the living, holy God among his people at these services?"[16] Both Saliers and Davis implicitly suggest the importance, value and imperative of communal worship experiences, while also explicitly connoting that there is much to be desired, quite often, as we seek and respond to "an engagement with him [God] on the terms that he [God] proposes and in the way that he [God] alone makes possible."[17] This is, of course, only relevant if we agree with W. Nicholls' articulation of worship in *Jacob's Ladder: The Meaning of Worship*, where he writes:

> Worship is the supreme and only indispensable activity of the Christian Church. It alone will endure, like the love for God which it expresses, into heaven, when all other activities of the Church will have passed away. It must therefore, even more strictly than any of the less essential doings of the Church, come under the criticism and control of the revelation on which the Church is founded.[18]

In times of sorrow and suffering, our communal worship must reflect—to the extent possible across numerous congregations—an active engagement of lament on behalf of both, the few, and the many. Learned from the many expressions of lament exemplified by the prophets of old and apostles of new, these four rituals are sorely needed in the church today: an honest complaint, a vulnerable plea, a transparent confession, and a song of praise.

## An Honest Complaint

In times of suffering, despair, and tragedy, the importance of an honest complaint is truly realized. As Rah recognizes, "Unfettered suffering devastates a fragile soul and a fragile community."[19] Yet the New Testament church is mandated to pray for one another, fellowship with one another, encourage one another, serve one another, and love one another.[20] Our communal gatherings cannot truthfully endeavor an engagement "in spirit and in truth" if we are not willing to offer honest complaint to God on behalf of one another.

Jeremiah's heart broke for his beloved people who continually rejected God's invitation to engage in an intimate relationship. As much as his anger was offered as a complaint to God in his heart-wrenching laments, Jeremiah's greatest complaint was against sin and evil—not necessarily against the people or God. Jeremiah, in his anger and rage, was still honest to the fact that sin and evil operate on and through people as a force, a negative power of sorts. People certainly become agents through which sin and evil occur, but the true source of Jeremiah's anger and the ultimate subject of his complaint was sin and evil.

Current sociopolitical posturing and platforms displace the subject of anger, creating a dishonest complaint. Far too often, the agents of sinful activities and evil actions are the source of the anger and the subject of the complaint, rather than the sinful nature of the actor and evil intervention from the perpetrator. In these situations, forgiveness, grace, compassion, and empathy are extremely difficult to invoke. Furthermore, our mischaracterization of our complaint, and our misalignment of the impact of sin and influence of evil, negates our ability to "humble ourselves, pray, seek God's face, and turn from our own wicked ways" (see 2 Chron. 7:14). It is too easy to acknowledge ourselves as in "the right" and non-likeminded people as in "the wrong," which inhibits our desire and ability to pray for one another, fellowship with one another, encourage one another, serve one another, and love one another as Jesus did. In this dishonest state, it is difficult to offer enough forgiveness, grace, compassion, and empathy to "love one another as we love ourselves" (see John 13:34).

## A Vulnerable Plea

It is a humble posture of life that leads to the transition from a self-important plea for one's own sake to a vulnerable plea on behalf of others. Jesus gave his life that we might be free of the wages of sin (Rom. 6:23). His vulnerable plea served as a living testimony of the love of a friend. Regardless of our righteousness and holiness at the time, Jesus gave his life as a reflection of God's monumental love for us, with a caveat that we should do even greater things (John 14:12). Jesus' teachings to his disciples were essentially master classes on vulnerability for the sake of others as a reflection of God's love for all of us.

Perhaps the apostle Paul understood this best as he offered himself as a prisoner of the gospel for the sake of the message to all (see Eph. 3:1; 4:1; Philem. 1:1). His vulnerable plea, like that of Jesus, is that no matter the circumstances or situation, we might learn to trust God and keep the faith. Our ability to accomplish this on behalf of the many will inevitably shift our posture of praise, as well as our perception of self-importance, availing the seat of power to the one who is the recipient of our vulnerable plea—our God in heaven.

## A Transparent Confession

On the cross between two thieves and in front of a crowd of hecklers, hopeless mourners, silent spectators, and enraged yet mortified escapists, Jesus offers the words, "Father, forgive them, for they know not what they do" (Luke 23:34). Rather than attempting to discern the subject of Jesus' plea as a Good Friday homilist aiming to impress the congregation might aim to do, perhaps it is better to follow this example of a transparent confession on behalf of us all.

There are times when our sense of desperation and destitution render us inactive, useless, and motionless—when we are in a state of paralysis, frozen in a helpless and hopeless state. We are so worn with fear and void of courage that our silence is deafening. We are so enraged and mortified that we perpetuate the same division and obstructive behavior we aim to eradicate.

We can respond to Jesus' invitation only by transparent confession. In times of destitution and despair, our ability to confess our weariness, our fatigue, and our disobedience is the only opportunity to stay connected to God, even through our rage. As I often reflect, preach, and teach, God is ginormous (simultaneously giant and enormous) enough to engage our angst and rage so we can still remain in relationship with him. Our transparent confession speaks louder than our political meanderings or platform positions. From our hearts, heads, and hands, we bare our soul to God so that Jesus' invitation does not fall on unfertile ground.

## A Song of Praise

Similar to David's lament in Psalm 69, after the honest complaint, vulnerable plea, and transparent confession, our offering of a song of praise is the expressive element that most effectively signals the culmination of a cycle. The song of praise offers a unique opportunity to again shift from one impassioned voice to the tempestuous voices of many, together. The gift of congregational or communal singing is often misunderstood and undervalued because of the singular focus on the aesthetic value of singing; yet the vital aspect of congregational or communal singing is the unification of the many into one collective voice. When many hearts, souls, and voices are aggregated in that fashion, the pain of the few becomes the pain of the many and, simultaneously, the hope of the few becomes the hope of the many. The kinesthetic action of breathing together merges with the theological reflection of the text that offers shared practice and creates a transition from the individual to the collective in breath, in voice and in power. Here solitude and loneliness give way to the temporal empowerment of togetherness—a powerful encounter that brings healing without minimizing one's personal experience.

A song such as "There Is a Balm in Gilead" has tremendous impact as a solo; but when accomplished as a collective offering of praise during a time of sorrow, it has abundant life-giving power. The refrain offers a solution, a source of healing to the wounded and the sin-sick soul. This balm in Gilead brings *shalom* to all in need. The vocalists articulate a personal narrative of discouragement that is resolved by the presence of the Holy Spirit who offers revival to their souls. One can suggest that the song is meant for solo voice, and it certainly can be performed as such; but the second verse offers a conversational tone that invokes the presence of others in the narrative, aiding us in seeing, sensing, and understanding that our song of praise is most potent when there are others in conversation, in praise and in worship together!

Let us vow to no longer decline opportunities to lament together. Let us bring our complaints, pleas, confessions, and songs of praise to one another—that we might share them before an audience of One, with the divine hope that our God will bring us collective healing.

> There is a balm in Gilead, to make the wounded whole;
> There is a balm in Gilead, to heal the sin-sick soul.
>
> Sometimes I feel discouraged and think my work's in vain,
> And then the Holy Spirit revives my soul again.
>
> There is a balm in Gilead, to make the wounded whole;
> There is a balm in Gilead, to heal the sin-sick soul.
>
> If you cannot preach like Peter, if you cannot pray like Paul,
> You can tell the love of Jesus and say "He died for all."
>
> There is a balm in Gilead, to make the wounded whole;
> There is a balm in Gilead, to heal the sin-sick soul.[21]

# Notes

## Chapter 1

1. G. Geoffrey Harper and Kit Barker, eds., *Finding Lost Words: The Church's Right to Lament*, Australian College of Theology Monograph Series (Eugene, OR: Wipf & Stock, 2017), 2–3.

2. In "The Art of Lament," Nicholas Wolterstorff asks the following question: "Is it part of our good created nature to grieve when something to which we are attached dies or is destroyed, or is this part of our fallen nature? John Calvin thought it was part of our created nature, and so do I. 'Afflicted by disease,' Calvin writes, 'we shall both groan and be uneasy and pant after health; pressed by poverty, we shall be pricked by the arrows of care and sorrow; we shall be smitten by the pain of disgrace, contempt, injustice; at the funerals of our dear ones we shall weep the tears that are owed to our nature. . . . Our Lord and Master groaned and wept both over his own and others' misfortunes. And he taught his disciples in the same way' (*Institutes* III.viii.10)." Wolterstorff's own conclusion is that "a faith that incorporates grief is stronger and richer than a faith that sings only praise songs." Wolterstorff, "The Art of Lament," July 27, 2012, http://www.thebanner.org.

3. Rico G. Villanueva, *It's OK to Be Not OK: The Message of the Lament Psalms* (Manila: OMF Literature, 2012), 30–31.

4. Page H. Kelley, "Prayers of Troubled Saints," *Review & Expositor* 81 (1984): 381.

5. Kelley, "Prayers of Troubled Saints," 381.

6. J. Todd Billings, *Rejoicing in Lament: Wrestling with Incurable Cancer and Life in Christ* (Grand Rapids: Brazos, 2015), 21.

7. Billings, *Rejoicing in Lament*, 40–41.

8. There has been a resurgence of interest in lament studies, especially the book of Psalms and, more recently, Lamentations. For some of these more recent studies see, for example: Andrew Sloane, "Lament and the Journey of Doubt," *Christian Scholar's Review* 29, no. 1 (1999): 113–27; Matthew Boulton, "Forsaking God: A Theological Argument for

Christian Lamentation," *Scottish Journal of Theology* 55 (2002): 58–78; Sally A. Brown and Patrick D. Miller, eds., *Lament* (Louisville, KY: Westminster John Knox, 2005); Richard A. Hughes, "Lament, Death, and Destiny," *Society of Biblical Literature* 68 (New York: Peter Lang, 2004); Michael Card, *A Sacred Sorrow: Reaching Out to God in the Lost Language of Lament* (Colorado Springs: NavPress, 2005); William S. Morrow, *Protest against God: The Eclipse of a Biblical Tradition*, Hebrew Bible Monographs 4 (Sheffield: Sheffield Phoenix, 2006); Nancy C. Lee, *Lyrics of Lament: From Tragedy to Transformation* (Minneapolis: Fortress, 2010); Glenn Pemberton, *Hurting with God: Learning to Lament with the Psalms* (Abilene, TX: Abilene Christian University Press, 2012); and Harper and Barker, *Finding Lost Words*. On Lamentations, see Robin A. Parry, "The Ethics of Lament: Lamentations 1 as a Case Study," in J. G. McConville and Karl Möller, eds., *Reading the Law: Essays in Honour of Gordon J. Wenham*, The Library of Hebrew Bible/Old Testament Studies 461 (London: T & T Clark, 2007): 138–55; Robin A. Parry, ed., *Great Is Thy Faithfulness?: Reading Lamentations as Sacred Scripture* (Eugene: Wipf & Stock, 2011); Heath Thomas, *Poetry and Theology in the Book of Lamentations: The Aesthetics of an Open Text*, Hebrew Bible Monographs (Sheffield: Sheffield Phoenix, 2013).

9. Walter A. Brueggemann, "The Formfulness of Grief," *Interpretation: A Journal of Bible and Theology* 31 (1977): 263.

10. In relation to Habakkuk 1–2, for example, Heath Thomas comments that "the prophet cries out to God because of rebellion within his own people (Hab. 1:1–3), God's use of idolaters to achieve his purposes, and the attack of the enemy that will destroy the earth (Hab. 1:12–17). These prophetic complaints are not faith-less prayers but rather are faith-filled prayer, aware that only God can alleviate these distresses." Heath Thomas, "Suffering," in *Dictionary of the Old Testament: Prophets*, ed. Mark J. Boda and J. Gordon McConville (Downers Grove, IL: IVP, 2012), 763.

11. Claus Westermann, *The Structure of the Book of Job*, trans. C. A. Muenchow (Philadelphia: Fortress Press, 1977), 33. See, for example, Erhard S. Gerstenberger, *Psalms Part 1 with an Introduction to Cultic Poetry*, ed. Rolf Knierim and Gene M. Tucker, *The Forms of the Old Testament Literature*, vol. 14 (Grand Rapids: Eerdmans, 1988), 12.

12. Westermann, *Structure of the Book of Job*, 67. Gerstenberger, *Psalms Part 1*, 13, notes that "PLEA or PETITION for help, together with its negative counterpart IMPRECATION against enemies, forms the very heart of a complaint song. There is hardly one pertinent psalm (only Psalm 88 comes close) that omits this central element. In fact, all the other elements can be interpreted as preparing and supporting the petition."

13. Claus Westermann, *Elements of Old Testament Theology*, trans. Douglas W. Scott (Atlanta: John Knox, 1982), 169.
14. Herbert E. Hohenstein, "Oh Blessed Rage," *Current in Theology and Mission* 10, no. 3 (June 1983): 165.
15. The title of Psalm 88 ("A song. A psalm of the Sons of Korah. For the director of music. According to *mahalath leannoth*. A *maskil* of Heman the Ezrahite.") combines elements found in the titles to Psalms 87 ("Of the Sons of Korah. A psalm. A song.") and 89 ("A *maskil* of Ethan the Ezrahite."). See Gerald Henry Wilson, *The Editing of the Hebrew Psalter*, Society of Biblical Literature Dissertation Series 76 (Chico, CA: Scholars Press, 1985): 164–65, who suggests that it is a deliberate editorial linking of these psalms at the end of Book 3. On a complementary track, Robert C. Culley, "Psalm 88 among the Complaints," *Ascribe to the Lord*, ed. Lyle Eslinger and Glen Taylor, *Journal for the Study of the Old Testament*, Supplement Series 67 (Sheffield: Sheffield Academic Press, 1988): 289–302, observes that Psalm 88 has no statement of confidence or trust or a vow to praise. Yet he argues that, because in the other laments, "the expectation of the notion of rescue is so strong that the limited mention of it in Psalm 88 is enough to evoke it with something of the importance and power it has in many of the other psalms. . . . What is not explained by the psalm itself can be picked up from some of the others."
16. Francis I. Andersen, *Job: An Introduction and Commentary*, Tyndale Old Testament Commentaries (Downers Grove, IL: InterVarsity Press, 1976), 98. Daniel J. Simundson, *The Message of Job: A Theological Commentary*, Augsburg OT Studies (Minneapolis: Augsburg, 1986), 107, also observes that "Job had wanted to lament, but his friends wanted to argue theology." Herbert Anderson, "The Bible and Pastoral Care," in *The Bible in Pastoral Practice*, ed. Paul H. Ballard and Stephen R. Holmes (London: Darton, Longman and Todd, 2005), 195–211, at 208 comments that "contrary to what we may assume, the Bible makes room in the life of faith for daring complaint to God rather than declaring such prayer off limits."
17. J. R. R. Tolkien, *Lord of the Rings*, 1007, cited in Harper and Barker, *Finding Lost Words*, 1.
18. On this change, see Federico G. Villanueva, *"The Uncertainty of a Hearing": A Study of the Sudden Change of Mood in the Lament Psalms* (Leiden: Brill, 2008); and Daniel J. Estes, "The Transformation of Pain into Praise in the Individual Lament Psalms," *The Psalms: Language for All Seasons of the Soul*, ed. Andrew J. Schmutzer and David M. Howard Jr. (Chicago: Moody, 2013), 151–64.
19. For another example, see Lamentations 3. Here we also see despair ("darkness rather than light," v. 2; "he has barred my way with blocks of

stone," v. 7); a sense that all his affliction is from God (vv. 37–38), who is boldly accused (e.g., vv. 2–16); a movement from a sense of total abandonment by God (e.g., "he shuts out my prayer," v. 8); to an experience of being heard and helped (vv. 55–57); a request for his enemies to be punished, but also a recognition that this is God's responsibility, not his (vv. 58–66); a reminder in the end of the faithfulness and steadfast love of God (vv. 22–25, 31–33), as the basis for hope against hope (v. 21), but in such a way as not to deny the darkness of the experience. The key features of lament are thus here reproduced.

20. On those laments that deal with sin, see Pemberton, *Hurting with God*, 77–88.

21. Claus Westermann, "The Role of the Lament in the Theology of the Old Testament," *Interpretation* 28 (1974): 33.

22. Westermann, *Elements of Old Testament Theology*, 173: "Here, too, the decisive element is said in the book of Job: Job defends himself against the friends who want to press him into a confession of guilt."

23. Jerry L. Sittser, *A Grace Disguised* (Grand Rapids: Zondervan, 1996), 45. I owe this reference to Dr. Peter Lau.

24. John Goldingay, *Old Testament Theology: Volume 3, Israel's Life* (Downers Grove, IL: IVP, 2009), 681.

25. Daniel J. Simundson, *Faith under Fire: Biblical Interpretations of Suffering* (Minneapolis: Augsburg, 1980), 58–59.

26. Interestingly, Glenn Pemberton followed up his book on learning to lament (*Hurting with God*) with an exploration about how to move on in trust after lament. See Glenn Pemberton, *After Lament: Psalms for Learning to Trust Again* (Abilene, TX: Abilene Christian University Press, 2014).

27. Roland E. Murphy, "The Last Truth about God," *Review & Expositor* 99 (2002): 586.

28. Kathleen A. Farmer, "Psalms," in *The Women's Bible Commentary*, ed. Carol A. Newsom and Sharon H. Ringe (Louisville, KY: Westminster John Knox Press, 1992), 140.

29. Walter A. Brueggemann, "From Hurt to Joy, from Death to Life," *Interpretation* 28 (1974): 5.

30. Simundson, *Faith under Fire*, 59–60.

31. Desmond Tutu, quoted in Gustavo Gutiérrez, *On Job: God-Talk and the Suffering of the Innocent*, trans. Matthew J. O'Connell (Maryknoll: Orbis, 1987), xv.

32. Choon-Leong Seow, "Job," *Dictionary of Scripture and Ethics*, ed. Joel B. Green (Grand Rapids: Baker, 2011), 421.

33. Walter A. Brueggemann, *The Message of the Psalms*, Augsburg OT Studies (Minneapolis: Augsburg, 1984), 52.

34. G. Geoffrey Harper, "Lament and the Sovereignty of God: Theological Reflections of Psalm 88," in Harper and Barker, *Finding Lost Words*, 80–93 at 80–81.

35. Billings, *Rejoicing in Lament*, 58.

36. J. T. Butler, cited in Goldingay, *Old Testament Theology*, 696.

37. D. K. Burge, "Man of Sorrows, What a Name! The Place of Lament in the New Testament," in Harper and Barker, *Finding Lost Words*, 116–29 at 116–17.

38. Burge, "Man of Sorrows," 120.

39. Burge, "Man of Sorrows," 121: "The Gospels foster lament ('blessed are you who weep now, for you will be filled') to a crucified, lamenting Lord."

40. Burge, "Man of Sorrows," 126. Billings, *Rejoicing in Lament*, 58, also discerns lament-like language in 2 Cor. 5:2; Rom. 8:23, 26. Rebekah Eklund, *Jesus Wept: The Significance of Jesus' Laments in the New Testament*, Library of New Testament Studies (London: Bloomsbury / T & T Clark, 2015), 160, also suggests that Paul also links the language of lament to perseverance in 2 Corinthians (e.g., 2 Cor. 4:7–12).

41. Eklund, *Jesus Wept*, 158, notes that "Rev. 6.9–11 demonstrates that complaint is certainly not inconsequential for those awaiting God's justice."

42. At 170, Eklund, *Jesus Wept*, defines lament in the NT as "a persistent cry for salvation to the God who promises to save, in a situation of suffering or sin, in the confident hope that this God hears and responds to cries and acts *now* and *in the future* to make whole." She notes that Jesus "prayed and embodied lament." She sees lament (172) as "a training in non-passive patience, in a form of waiting that strains eagerly toward the future."

43. Keith Campbell, "Lament in James and Its Significance for the Church," *Journal of the Evangelical Theological Society* 60, no. 1 (2017): 125–38. Campbell's work could be extended further by seeing how James 5:11 links Job with persevering in faith. D. West, "The Shape and Function of New Testament Lament," in Harper and Barker, *Finding Lost Words*, 108–15. At 109–110, West notes that while lament is still used in the NT (Mark 14:36; 15:34; 2 Cor. 12:7–8; Rev. 6:9–11), there are three additions: the prayer promise of being heard, exhortation to keep on crying out to God for vindication in the midst of trial or struggle, and the willingness for God's will to happen. Burge, "Man of Sorrows," 116–29. Prior to 2014, see Keith Campbell, "NT Lament in Current Research and Its Implications for American Evangelicals," *Journal of the Evangelical Theological Society* 57, no. 4 (2014): 757–72.

44. M. J. Gill, "Praying Lament," in Harper and Barker, *Finding Lost Words*, 223–36 at 234.

45. Anderson, "The Bible and Pastoral Care," 195–211 at 208, comments that "the recovery of lament is a critical alternative to apathy in our time. Unless we learn to lament, we are powerless in the face of so much irrational suffering in the world. We are empowered when we lament. . . . The language of lament gives voice to mute pain and creates communities of the suffering ones."

46. Soong-Chan Rah, *Prophetic Lament: A Call for Justice in Troubled Times* (Downers Grove, IL: IVP, 2015), 2, notes that there can be a self-serving motivation behind avoiding lament. He writes that "Christian communities arising from celebration do not want their lives changed, because their lives are in a good place. . . . Lament recognizes the struggles of life and cries out for justice against existing injustices."

47. David J. Cohen, "'Why O Lord?' Lament as a Window to the Human Experience of Distress," in Harper and Barker, *Finding Lost Words*, 66–79 at 77.

48. Anderson, "The Bible and Pastoral care," 195–211 at 208, notes that "*Rachel's Cry,* subtitled *Prayer of Lament and the Recovery of Hope*, by pastoral theologian Kathleen D. Billman and systematic theologian Daniel L. Migliore (1999), is a compelling invitation to recover the prayer of lament as a way of hope in a time of irrational suffering and deepening despair. The question they ask is this: what guidance does the Bible and the theological tradition give us regarding the inclusion of lament as well as praise and thanksgiving in the practice of Christian living?"

49. Nancy J. Duff, "Recovering Lamentation as a Practice in the Church," in *Lament: Reclaiming Practices in Pulpit, Pew, and Public Square*, ed. Sally A. Brown and Patrick D. Miller (Louisville, KY: Westminster John Knox, 2005), 3–14 at 13.

# Chapter 2

1. For example, the Assur cylinder, various inscriptions, and the Babylonian Chronicles' mention of a city's fall and rise are texts that span over time (1600–500 BC).

2. The city lament genre was generated from around 2000 to 1600 BC in Mesopotamia. The texts include five historical city laments: *The Lamentation over Sumer and Ur*, the *Lamentation over the Destruction of Ur*, the *Eridu Lament*, the *Uruk Lament*, and the *Nippur Lament*. Each lament details a specific historical event of the devastation of major cities at the collapse of the Third Ur Dynasty around 1925 BC. In the first millennium, one finds the literary descendants of the historical laments. These

are known as *balags* and *ersemmas*. The *balags* and *ersemmas* also lament a major public disaster affecting the temple, city, or entire land. These appear as early as 1900 BC (Old Babylonian Period) with redactions dating to the Seleucid period. When we speak of the city lament, therefore, we are speaking of an enduring literary genre.

    3. F. W. Dobbs-Allsopp, *Weep, O Daughter of Zion: A Study of the City-Lament Genre in the Hebrew Bible*, Biblica Et Orientalia 44 (Roma: Editrice Pontificio Istituto Biblico, 1993).

    4. For a thorough study on the topic of lament features in the book of Ezekiel, see Donna Lee Petter, *The Book of Ezekiel and Mesopotamian City Laments*, Orbis Biblicus Et Orientalis (Fribourg: Academic Press, 2011), 246. See also Donna Petter, "Notes on Ezekiel," *NIV Zondervan Study Bible: New International Version*, ed. D. A. Carson (Grand Rapids: Zondervan, 2015).

    5. Said another way, the well-known themes running through Ezekiel associated with covenantal curses (such as death, destruction, abandonment, and anger of God) converge in the literary framework of the city lament. Although Ezekiel utilizes the city lament and associated motifs for mourning the dead, he has adapted it for his own frame of reference, the covenantal framework, and the venue whereby he understood Yahweh's interactions with his people. This is not unlike Mosaic reliance and use of ancient Near East law and Hittite suzerainty treaties in the production of Exodus and Deuteronomy (Covenantal Law). He relies on standard literary motifs of a destroyed city for their conceptual framework but fills the old pattern with new content to suit his context. He adapts and modifies the city lament features in creative ways. See Petter, *The Book of Ezekiel and Mesopotamian City Laments*.

    6. To be sure, Psalm 137 shows that while in Babylon the exiles did weep as they remembered their homeland, but not necessarily for sin. God's people did experience remorse over sin based on what we know from the book of Lamentations, but this sentiment comes *after* the city fell.

    7. Although she offers a different interpretation of the event, credit goes to Margaret Odell for the use of this well-known phrase relative to Ezekiel 2:8–9. See "You Are What You Eat: Ezekiel and the Scroll Incident," *Journal of Biblical Literature* (January 1, 1998).

    8. See Petter, *The Book of Ezekiel and Mesopotamian City Laments*.

    9. In fact, mourning after the news of the fall would not have been appropriate. For further explanation, see Petter, *The Book of Ezekiel and Mesopotamian City Laments*, 69–73.

    10. See Lindsay Wilson, "Lament as a Prayer of Faith," chapter 1 in this book.

    11. Petter, *The Book of Ezekiel and Mesopotamian City Laments*.

12. To be sure, select psalms do offer lamentation specifically for sin at both the individual (Pss. 32, 38, 51, 130, 143) and communal levels (Pss. 4, 60, 74, 79, 80, 83, 89).

13. Unlike Job, Ezra was not forced into a confession of guilt. His knowledge of Torah, along with his priestly role, likely accounts for his appropriate response. With Job, there is no relationship between lament and confession of sin (see Wilson in this book).

14. See Sean McDonough, "Lament in the New Testament," chapter 4 in this book. Cf. Laurie J. Braaten, "All Creation Groans: Romans 8:22 in Light of the Biblical Sources," *Horizons in Biblical Theology* 28 (2006): 131–59.

15. There is the tension, however, between the now and the not-yet due to the cross. For while it can be argued that we are in at time of mourning during our exile on earth, we have been adorned with festival garments and white robes of victory (a new relationship has been established), so it is also a time to rejoice as we await the bridegroom, as we await the divine presence.

# Chapter 3

1. Scott H. Hendrix, *Recultivating the Vineyard: The Reformation Agendas of Christianization* (Louisville, KY: Westminster John Knox Press, 2004), 11, 14, 66.

2. Rhys S. Bezzant, "*Semper Reformanda*: The Revivalists and the Reformers," in *Celebrating the Reformation: Its Legacy and Continuing Relevance*, ed. M. D. Thompson, C. Bale, and E. Loane (London: Apollos, 2017). See also Rachel Ciano, "Lament Psalms in the Church: A History of Recent Neglect," in *Finding Lost Words: The Church's Right to Lament*, ed. G. Geoffrey Harper and Kit Barker (Eugene, OR: Wipf and Stock, 2017).

3. See W. Reginald Ward, *The Protestant Evangelical Awakening* (Cambridge: University Press, 1992).

4. Tom Schwanda, ed. *The Emergence of Evangelical Spirituality: The Age of Edwards, Newton, and Whitefield*, The Classics of Western Spirituality (New York: Paulist Press, 2016), 74–75, 123, 178, 231.

5. Oliver D. Crisp, *Jonathan Edwards among the Theologians* (Grand Rapids: Eerdmans, 2015), 146–51.

6. Jonathan Edwards, "The Dangers of Decline," in *Sermons and Discourses, 1730–1733*, The Works of Jonathan Edwards 17, ed. M. Valeri (New Haven: Yale University Press, 1999), 97, 99.

7. Ian J. Maddock, "A Song Once Known: The Use of Psalm 77 by Calvin, Henry, Wesley, and Simeon," in Harper and Barker, *Finding Lost Words*, 33–35.

8. Nathan O. Hatch, *The Democratization of American Christianity* (New Haven: Yale University Press, 1989).
9. Todd M. Brenneman, *Homespun Gospel: The Triumph of Sentimentality in Contemporary American Evangelicalism* (New York: Oxford University Press, 2014), 9.
10. Brenneman, *Homespun Gospel*, 7, 15.
11. Stephen Marini, "Hymnody as History: Early Evangelical Hymns and the Recovery of American Popular Religion," *Church History* 71, no. 2 (2002): 273–306, esp. 302.
12. "How Great Thou Art," hymn written by Swedish composer Carl Boberg in 1885 and translated into English by Stuart K. Hine in 1949.
13. See D. W. Whittle in Timothy George, ed., *Mr. Moody and the Evangelical Tradition* (London: T & T Clark, 2004), 85–86.
14. Donald E. Hall, "Muscular Christianity: Reading and Writing the Male Social Body," in *Muscular Christianity: Embodying the Victorian Age*, ed. Donald E. Hall (Cambridge: Cambridge University Press, 1994), 7, 9.
15. As quoted in Randall Balmer, *Blessed Assurance: A History of Evangelicalism in America* (Boston: Beacon Press, 1999), 86.
16. Balmer, *Blessed Assurance*, 91.
17. Randall Balmer, *The Making of Evangelicalism: From Revivalism to Politics and Beyond* (Waco, TX: Baylor University Press, 2010), 36.
18. Kate Bowler, *Blessed: A History of the American Prosperity Gospel* (New York: Oxford University Press, 2013), 7.
19. Bowler, *Blessed*, 20.
20. Matthew Avery Sutton, *American Apocalypse: A History of Modern Evangelicalism* (Cambridge, MA: The Belknap Press of Harvard University Press, 2014), 5.
21. Sutton, *American Apocalypse*, 59.
22. Sutton, *American Apocalypse*, 95. See also Philip Jenkins, *The Great and Holy War: How World War I Became a Religious Crusade* (New York: HarperOne, 2014).
23. Rhys S. Bezzant, *Standing on their Shoulders: Heroes of the Faith for Today* (Brunswick: Acorn, 2015), 94–95.
24. Grant Wacker, *America's Pastor: Billy Graham and the Shaping of a Nation* (Cambridge, MA: The Belknap Press of Harvard University Press, 2014), 17.
25. Wacker, *America's Pastor*, 99.
26. Matthew Everhard, "Interview with Robert Caldwell: Author of *Theologies of the American Revivalists*," *Jonathan Edward Studies*, May 24, 2017, https://edwardsstudies.com/2017/05/24/interview-with-robert-caldwell-author-of-theologies-of-the-american-revivalists/.

# Chapter 4

1. Scripture references taken from the NIV unless otherwise noted.
2. Many thanks to Rachel Danley for her assistance in undertaking the research for this article.
3. Cf. Martin Ebner, "Klage und Auferweckungshoffnung im Neuen Testament," in *Klage, Jahrbuch für Biblische Theologie* 16 (Neukirchen-Vluyn: Neukirchener, 2001): 73–87.
4. See Rebekah Eklund, *Jesus Wept: The Significance of Jesus' Laments in the New Testament*, Library of New Testament Studies (London: Bloomsbury / T & T Clark, 2015).
5. Discerning precise examples of early Christian hymns can be difficult, but there is little doubt they were used in churches. See, for example, Jack T. Sanders, *The New Testament Christological Hymns* (Cambridge: Cambridge University Press, 2004).
6. One might begin a survey of lament in the New Testament with Bernhard Anderson's list of verses from Old Testament laments used in the NT in his indispensable *Out of the Depths: The Psalms Speak for Us Today*, with Steven Bishop, 3rd ed. (Louisville, KY: Westminster John Knox Press, 2000), 224–28. Anderson offers over fifty instances in which the NT quotes or alludes to OT lament psalms. One can always debate whether a given psalm on the list should qualify as a "lament." Psalm 90, for instance, has aspects of lament to it, but one might easily categorize it as a "wisdom" psalm. Anderson also makes it clear that many of these verses are not deployed as laments by the NT writers; thus 2 Peter 3:8 uses Ps. 90:4 ("With the Lord a day is like a thousand years and a thousand years is like a day") as an expression of trust. Nevertheless, he has demonstrated at a minimum that these psalms played an active role in the life of the early church.
7. See Ebner, 81ff. He shows how miracle stories actually serve the lament theme quite well, since OT laments work toward faith in God based on his past acts. Thus sufferers take heart from the miracle story even as they still find themselves in the role of present lamenters. Ebner further notes that since OT lament may be based on the ongoing relevance of the Exodus events, the echoes of Exodus in the NT warrant a similar deployment of lament.
8. Ebner, 86.
9. Ebner, 86.
10. Gail O'Day, "Surprised by Faith: Jesus and the Canaanite Woman," *Listening* 24 (1989): 290–301. See the discussion in Eklund, 18–20, and Ellington, 175–78.
11. Ebner, 75–81.

12. Matthew records Jesus speaking these words in the midst of his final week, while Luke includes the words as Jesus makes his way to Jerusalem. In any event, the looming destruction of the city is evident in both accounts. For OT background for the lament, see David Pao and Eckhard J. Schnabel, "Luke," in *Commentary on the New Testament Use of the Old Testament*, ed. G. K. Beale and D. A. Carson (Grand Rapids: Baker, 2007), at Luke 13:31–35.

13. Eklund, 25–36.

14. For a detailed discussion of the use of Psalm 42 here, see Eklund, 32–34.

15. Eklund, 36.

16. See Ebner, 75–81. Ebner puts Mark's version of the cry of dereliction at the center of his justification for NT lament. He notes that Mark in effect presents the elements of Psalm 22, with Jesus' citation of v. 2 as the climax of the motif. Ebner offers strong arguments against those who would say that Jesus' citation of Psalm 22 implies the positive affirmation of trust at the end of the psalm.

17. See Ebner, 75–81; Matthew Rindge, "Reconfiguring the Akedah and Recasting God: Lament and Divine Abandonment in Mark," *Journal of Biblical Literature* 130, no. 1 (2011): 755–74.

18. Karl Barth, *Church Dogmatics* IV/1 (Peabody, MA: Hendrickson, 2010): 215.

19. Note the double mention of the Sabbath in the ensuing verse, and the fact that the John's Gospel begins by citing Christ's role in creation and continues with repeated reference to his "work" for the Father (see, e.g., 5:17, 20; 7:3; 9:3; 10:25; 14:10; 15:24).

20. For discussion, see D. A. Carson, *The Gospel According to John* (Grand Rapids: Eerdmans, 1991), 618–20.

21. For discussion, see Stuhlmacher, "Klage und Dank," in *Klage*, 55–72.

22. Laurie J. Braaten, "All Creation Groans: Romans 8:22 in Light of the Biblical Sources," *Horizons in Biblical Theology* 28 (2006): 131–59; cf. Markus Öhler, "To Mourn, Weep, Lament, and Groan," in *Evoking Lament: A Theological Discussion* (London: T&T Clark, 2009): 150–66, esp. 154ff.

23. For a detailed discussion, see David Starling, "'For Your Sake We Are Being Killed All Day Long': Romans 8:36 and the Hermeneutics of Unexplained Suffering," *Themelios* 42, no. 1 (2017): 112–21.

24. Paul goes on later in the Epistle to show how Timothy and Epaphroditus also imitate Christ as he is presented in the hymn of chapter 2.

25. Cf. Donna Petter, "Lament in the Book of Ezekiel: Its Purpose and Function," in chapter 2 of this book, and Eklund, 12–16.

26. See Luke Timothy Johnson, *The Letter of James*, Anchor Bible 37A (New York: Doubleday, 1995), 302–3. For a more involved discussion, see Keith Campbell, "Lament in James and Its Significance for the Church," *Journal of the Evangelical Theological Society* 60, no. 1 (2017): 125–38.

27. For a thorough treatment of this verse, see Rainer Schwindt, "Der Klageruf der Märtyer," *Biblische Notizen* NF 141 (2009): 117–36; NF 142 (2009): 119–30.

28. There is yet more irony here when we recognize that the phrase translated "as they deserve" (ἄξιοί εἰσιν) is more literally rendered "they are worthy." This is an obvious counterpoint to the divine acclamation, "You are worthy" (ἄξιος εἶ) in, for example, 4:11 and 5:9.

# Chapter 5

1. On a personal note, I would like to thank Lindsay Wilson and Rhys Bezzant for embodying the kinds of care I mention in this essay. My thanks for helpful feedback for this paper go to Andrew Malone and Anne Ellison from Ridley College and also those who participated in the Ridley/Gordon-Conwell conference on lament, especially Adonis Vidu. This essay engages 2 Corinthians with some of the core ideas I expand on, with special attention to Matthew's Gospel, in *God of All Comfort: A Trinitarian Response to the Horrors of This World* (Bellingham, WA: Lexham Press, 2019).

2. Nathaniel A. Carlson, "Lament: The Biblical Language of Trauma," *Cultural Encounters* 11, no. 1 (2015): 50.

3. Ibid., 56. Italics are original.

4. Keith Campbell, "NT Scholars' Use of OT Lament Terminology and Its Theological and Interdisciplinary Implications," *Bulletin for Biblical Research* 21, no. 2 (2011): 217. For the purposes of this project, it is important to note that there are strong continuities and discontinuities between OT and NT laments. The theological assumptions driving OT laments include faith in God's righteousness and power: God's righteousness that drives the idea that he wills justice and also acts for justice, and God's power that secures his ability to overcome the enemies of the lamenter and also to change the particular situation at hand. Though there are strong continuities between OT and NT beliefs concerning God's righteousness and power, profound theological discontinuities between OT and NT writers strongly shape the nature and practice of NT laments. NT laments occur within unique Trinitarian and eschatological horizons.

5. Keith Campbell, "NT Lament in Current Research and Its Implications for American Evangelicals," *Journal of the Evangelical Theological Society* 57, no. 4 (2014): 767–68.

6. Ibid. These criteria still apply even if the exhaustive content and circumstances of the lament remain undisclosed.

7. Andrew Hassler, "Glimpses of Lament: 2 Corinthians and the Presence of Lament in the New Testament," *Journal of Spiritual Formation and Soul Care* 9, no. 2 (2016): 167.

8. Ibid.

9. Ibid.

10. Ibid., 175. Hassler draws on Ellington and Eklund's work. Scott A. Ellington, *Risking Truth: Reshaping the World through Prayers of Lament*, Princeton Theological Monograph Series 98 (Eugene, OR: Pickwick, 2008); Rebekah Eklund, *Jesus Wept: The Significance of Jesus' Laments in the New Testament*, The Library of New Testament Studies (London: Bloomsbury T & T Clark, 2015).

11. Hassler, "Glimpses of Lament," 167.

12. Ibid., 175. Hassler's work is consistent with Campbell's criteria. Campbell, "NT Lament in Current Research," 767–68.

13. All Bible references taken from the Christian Standard Bible.

14. Harris notes that "similar catalogues of hardships [to those found in 2 Corinthians] are found in Rom. 8:35–39; 1 Cor. 4:9–13; 2 Cor. 6:4–10; 11:23–28; 12:10; Phil. 4:11–12." Murray J. Harris, *The Second Epistle to the Corinthians*, The New International Greek Testament Commentary (Grand Rapids: Eerdmans, 2005), 341.

15. American Psychiatric Association, *Diagnostic and Statistical Manual of Mental Disorders: DSM-5* (Washington, DC: American Psychiatric Association, 2013), 830, cited in Carlson, "Lament," 50.

16. Charles A. Schaefer and Frauke C. Schaefer, eds., *Trauma and Resilience: A Handbook* (n.p.: Frauke C. Shaefer, MD, Inc., 2016), vi.

17. Kathleen M. O'Connor, *Jeremiah: Pain and Promise* (Minneapolis: Fortress, 2012), 3. This is not a new phenomenon; see, for example, the Late Medieval metaphors for perception and its obstacles in the midst of suffering (e.g., the uses of "night," "wall," and "ladder").

18. Shelly Rambo, "Spirit and Trauma," *Interpretation: A Journal of Bible and Theology* 69, no. 1 (2014): 8 (italics original).

19. Serene Jones, *Trauma and Grace: Theology in a Ruptured World* (Louisville, KY: Westminster John Knox, 2009), viii (italics original).

20. Although Stump's approach to this is similar to mine in some respects, there are important differences between us. See Eleonore Stump, "Atonement and the Cry of Dereliction from the Cross," *European Journal for Philosophy of Religion* 4, no. 1 (2012): 1–17. Stump trades primarily on

the notion of union stemming from a "mind-reading" type of the physical theory of the atonement; ibid., 14. In addition, I don't accept her account of love stated aside from holiness and its systematic consequences for God's closeness to all people; ibid., 5. Though I appreciate that Christ may experience the ugliness of the sin of those he knows (Matt. 7:21–23), I struggle to understand the warrant for a two-way psychic closeness between Christ's mind and the minds of all people; ibid., 16–17. Though I agree that "accessibility to the psyche of Christ might be a great redemptive good for human beings," I cannot see how this may occur without an account of the Holy Spirit's work; ibid., 17

21. Stump, "Atonement," 8.
22. Ibid.
23. Ibid.
24. Ibid., 2. Stump continues: "Closeness is necessary for the union sought in love. . . . [T]his ability and willingness to share oneself in turn require psychic integration."
25. Eleonore Stump, "Narrative and the Knowledge of Persons," *Euresis Journal* 5 (2013): 153–69; Eleonore Stump, *Wandering in Darkness: Narrative and the Problem of Suffering* (Oxford: Oxford University Press, 2010); Thomas V. Morris, *The Logic of God Incarnate* (Ithaca, NY: Cornell University Press, 1986).
26. Morris, *The Logic of God Incarnate*.
27. Marion Hourdequin, "Empathy, Shared Intentionality, and Motivation by Moral Reasons," *Ethical Theory and Moral Practice* 15, no. 3 (2012): 411 (italics original).
28. Adam Green, "Reading the Mind of God (without Hebrew Lessons): Alston, Shared Attention, and Mystical Experience," *Religious Studies* 45, no. 4 (2009): 459.
29. Ibid.
30. Stump writes about fragmentedness with respect to moral evil and closeness between persons. Stump, "Atonement," 2–3.
31. Ibid., 11.
32. Contra Harris, for whom this is not a uniquely Christian description of God. He seems to ignore the context when he writes: "Paul is reproducing, without any explicit Christian addition, a common Semitic description of God, found notably in the second prayer of the 'Eighteen Benedictions,' which were recited two or three times each day in synagogue worship." Harris, *Second Epistle to the Corinthians*, 157. For Paul, the only true God is the one who raised Jesus Christ, God the Son. In 1 Cor. 15:13–15, Paul writes: "If Christ has not been raised, then our proclamation is in vain, and so is your faith. Moreover, we are found to be false witnesses about God, because we have testified wrongly about God that he raised up Christ."

33. Guy Bonneau, "À la vie, À la mort: Le conflit à Corinthe et ses enjeux théologiques en 2 Co 2,14–7,4," *Science et Esprit* 51, no. 3 (1999): 360.

34. Ibid., 365. Paul's central request to the Corinthians in 6:14–7:4 is that they may find a place for Paul in their heart (7:2–4).

35. Charles Journet and Fondation Cardinal Journet, *Notre Père qui es aux cieux: retraite doctrinale* (Paris: Desclée de Brouwer, 1987); Charles Journet, *Entretiens sur Dieu le Père* (Saint-Maur: Parole et silence, 1998); Charles Journet, *Entretiens sur l'espérance* (Saint-Maur: Parole et silence: Diffusion Cerf, 1998); Charles Journet, *Entretiens sur le Saint-Esprit* (Saint-Maur: Parole et Silence, 1997).

36. Charles Journet, *The Church of the Word Incarnate* (London: Sheed and Ward, 1955); Charles Journet, *The Theology of the Church* (San Francisco: Ignatius Press, 2004); Charles Journet, *The Mass: The Presence of the Sacrifice of the Cross* (South Bend, IN: St Augustine's Press, 2008). My thanks go to Adonis Vidu for a conversation on Journet. The work of Giles Emery will also be beneficial to this project. Emery, *Trinity, Church, and the Human Person: Thomistic Essays* (Naples, FL: Sapientia Press of Ave Maria University, 2007).

# Chapter 6

1. All Bible references taken from the English Standard Version.

2. Established by an Act of the United States Congress in 2003, the National Museum of African American History & Culture opened to the public on September 24, 2016. The nineteenth museum of the Smithsonian Institute is "the only national museum devoted exclusively to the documentation of African American life, history and culture." Central to the museum's numerous exhibitions is an experiential and interactive journey through the complex narrative of slavery and freedom beginning in fifteenth-century Africa and Europe, extending to twenty-first-century United States.

3. Michael E. Ruane, "Haunting Relics from a Slave Ship Headed for African American Museum," *The Washington Post*, July 13, 2016.

4. Ibid.

5. Ibid.

6. Paul Leroy Robeson was a twice-named All-American scholar-athlete and valedictorian at Rutgers College, and a graduate of Columbia Law School. Born in 1898, the Princeton, New Jersey, native achieved great acclaim during the Negro renaissance in Harlem as a concert bass baritone and actor. His political activism against racism and lynching, as well as his advocacy for the liberation of colonized African nations, earned

him the status of officially "blacklisted" by the United States Government, availing even more meaning to his performance of Negro spirituals.

7. Soong-Chan Rah, *Prophetic Lament: A Call for Justice in Troubled Times* (Downers Grove, IL: InterVarsity Press, 2015).

8. Ibid., 9.

9. For scriptural references, see Gen. 1–2:4; Ps. 11:1; 46:1–3; John 4:31–34; and Matt 6:25–34.

10. This is an adaptation of Jude 1:24.

11. Papal bulls are pontifical decrees issued by the pope of the Roman Catholic Church. Under the authority of Pope Alexander VI (papacy 1492–1503), a number of papal bulls substantiated the age of discovery leading to the colonization of non-Christian lands. The combination of select papal bulls, the 1494 Treaty of Tordesillas, and the policies of Secretary of State Thomas Jefferson in 1792 institutionalized within the United States the Doctrine of Discovery, which also gave rise to colonization and decimation of generations of indigenous peoples in the West and Global South. To read more, see Robert J. Miller and Elizabeth Forse, *Native America, Discovered and Conquered: Thomas Jefferson, Lewis & Clark, and Manifest Destiny* (Westport, CT: Praeger Publishers, 2006); Robert J. Miller, Jacinta Ruru, Larissa Behrendt, and Tracey Lindberg, *Discovering Indigenous Lands: The Doctrine of Discovery in the English Colonies* (New York: Oxford University Press, 2010); also see the assorted works of Mark Charles.

12. On August 24, 1955, Chicago native Emmett Louis Till stopped in Bryant's Grocery and Meat Market with his cousins and a few local boys while visiting family in Money, Mississippi. Although numerous versions of the account exist, the dominant narrative was from the store owner, Carolyn Bryant, who claimed that fourteen-year-old Emmett whistled at her, grabbed her hand, and propositioned her for a date. On August 28, between 2:00 and 3:30 AM, Till was kidnapped from his uncle's home and lynched. His maimed body was tied to a seventy-pound cotton gin fan and discarded in the Tallahatchie River.

After receiving Till's body in Chicago, his mother, Mamie Till Bradley, held an open casket funeral with Till's mutilated body on full display for mourners and the media. The photos from the open casket and the reaction from the grand jury's decision not to indict the named kidnappers served as a tipping point for a national civil rights movement burgeoning in the South.

Recent research reveals Carolyn Bryant's admission that she made up the sensational details of the August 24 event that caused the horrific murder of an innocent teenager. For more, read Devery S. Anderson, *Emmett Till: The Murder That Shocked the World and Propelled the Civil Rights*

*Movement* (Jackson: University Press of Mississippi, 2015); and Timothy B. Tyson, *The Blood of Emmett Till* (New York: Simon & Schuster, 2017).

13. Fifteen sticks of dynamite were detonated by a timing device under the east stairwell of the historic Baptist church in Birmingham, Alabama, killing Addie Mae Collins (14), Carol Denise McNair (11), Carole Robertson (14), and Cynthia Wesley (14). Fifty-two years later, Cynthia Marie Graham Hurd, Susie Jackson, Ethel Lee Lance, Depayne Middleton-Doctor, Tywanza Sanders, Daniel L. Simmons, Sharonda Coleman-Singleton, Myra Thompson, and senior pastor and state senator Clementa C. Pinckney were murdered in the historic African Methodist Episcopal Church in Charleston, South Carolina, during a prayer service. Their ages ranged from 26 to 87.

14. Don E. Saliers, *Worship Come to Its Senses* (Nashville: Abingdon Press, 1996).

15. Ibid., 14.

16. John Jefferson Davis, *Worship and the Reality of God: An Evangelical Theology of Real Presence* (Downers Grove, IL: IVP Academic, 2010), 9.

17. David Peterson, *Engaging with God: A Biblical Theology of Worship* (Downers Grove, IL: IVP Academic, 1992), 20. This is Peterson's definition of Christian worship.

18. Quoted in Peterson, 15. The original text is published by Lutterworth Press (1958) as part of the Ecumenical Studies in Worship Series.

19. Rah, *Prophetic Lament*, 112.

20. Over fifty scriptures in the New Testament admonish the church to do unto "one another." A sample of such are: James 5:16; Rom. 12:16; 13:8; 1 Pet. 4:8–9; 1 Thess. 4:18; 5:11; Gal. 5:13; John 13:34–35; and 1 John 4:11–12.

21. Although the first published version of this traditional African American spiritual was attributed to Washington Blass ("The Sinner's Cure," 1854), there is no known composer. Like most spirituals, the text has been passed from generation to generation through oral tradition, often with variations and multiple simultaneous versions interpreted across various regions of the country and world.

Of importance to this text is the New Testament response to the Old Testament questions stemming from Jeremiah 8:22, "Is there no balm in Gilead? Is there no physician there? Why then has the health of the daughters of my people not been restored?" The refrain addresses these three questions by asserting that, indeed, there is a balm in Gilead in the love of God, the passion of Christ, and the presence of the Holy Spirit.

This text comes from Paul Robeson's historic May 9, 1958, Carnegie Hall performance (Alan Booth, piano) as recorded by Vanguard Records and released in 1960, 1965, 1987, and 2006.

# Bibliography

Andersen, Francis I. *Job: An Introduction and Commentary*. Tyndale Old Testament Commentaries. Downers Grove, IL: InterVarsity, 1976.

Anderson, Bernhard, and Steven Bishop. *Out of the Depths: The Psalms Speak for Us Today*. 3rd ed. Louisville, KY: Westminster John Knox, 2000.

Anderson, Devery S. *Emmett Till: The Murder That Shocked the World and Propelled the Civil Rights Movement*. Jackson: University Press of Mississippi, 2015.

Anderson, Herbert. "The Bible and Pastoral Care." In *The Bible in Pastoral Practice: Readings in the Place and Function of Scripture in the Church*. Edited by Paul H. Ballard and Stephen R. Holmes. Using the Bible in Pastoral Practice. London: Darton, Longman and Todd, 2005.

Balmer, Randall. *Blessed Assurance: A History of Evangelicalism in America*. Boston: Beacon, 1999.

———. *The Making of Evangelicalism: From Revivalism to Politics and Beyond*. Waco, TX: Baylor University Press, 2010.

Barber II, William J., with Jonathan Wilson-Hartgrove. *The Third Reconstruction: Moral Mondays, Fusion Politics, and the Rise of a New Justice Movement*. Boston: Beacon, 2016.

Barth, Karl. *Church Dogmatics* IV/1. Peabody, MA: Hendrickson, 2010.

Bezzant, Rhys S. "Semper Reformanda: The Revivalists and the Reformers." In *Celebrating the Reformation: Its Legacy and Continuing Relevance*. Edited by Mark D. Thompson, Colin Bale, and Edward Loane, 309–28. London: Apollos, 2017.

———. *Standing on Their Shoulders: Heroes of the Faith for Today*. Brunswick: Acorn, 2015.

Billings, J. Todd. *Rejoicing in Lament: Wrestling with Incurable Cancer and Life in Christ.* Grand Rapids: Brazos, 2015.

Birch, Bruce C. *Let Justice Roll Down: The Old Testament, Ethics, and Christian Life.* Louisville, KY: Westminster / John Knox, 1991.

Bonneau, Guy. "À la vie, À la mort: Le conflit à Corinthe et ses enjeux théologiques en 2 Co 2,14–7,4." *Science et Esprit* 51, no. 3 (1999).

Boulton, Matthew. "Forsaking God: A Theological Argument for Christian Lamentation." *Scottish Journal of Theology* 55 (2002).

Bowler, Kate. *Blessed: A History of the American Prosperity Gospel.* New York: Oxford University Press, 2013.

Braaten, Laurie J. "All Creation Groans: Romans 8:22 in Light of the Biblical Sources." *Horizons in Biblical Theology* 28 (2006).

Brenneman, Todd M. *Homespun Gospel: The Triumph of Sentimentality in Contemporary American Evangelicalism.* New York: Oxford University Press, 2014.

Brown, Sally A., and Patrick D. Miller, eds. *Lament: Reclaiming Practices in Pulpit, Pew, and Public Square.* Louisville, KY: Westminster John Knox, 2005.

Brueggemann, Walter A. "The Formfulness of Grief." *Interpretation: A Journal of Bible and Theology* 31 (1977).

———. "From Hurt to Joy, from Death to Life." *Interpretation: A Journal of Bible and Theology* 28 (1974).

———. *The Message of the Psalms.* Augsburg OT Studies. Minneapolis: Augsburg, 1984.

Campbell, Keith. "Lament in James and Its Significance for the Church." *Journal of the Evangelical Theological Society* 60, no. 1 (2017).

———. "NT Lament in Current Research and Its Implications for American Evangelicals." *Journal of the Evangelical Theological Society* 57, no. 4 (2014).

———. "NT Scholars' Use of OT Lament Terminology and Its Theological and Interdisciplinary Implications." *Bulletin for Biblical Research* 21, no. 2 (2011).

Card, Michael. *A Sacred Sorrow: Reaching Out to God in the Lost Language of Lament.* Colorado Springs: NavPress, 2005.

Carlson, Nathaniel A. "Lament: The Biblical Language of Trauma." *Cultural Encounters* 11, no. 1 (2015).

Carson, D. A. *The Gospel According to John*. Grand Rapids: Eerdmans, 1991.

———, ed. *Worship by the Book*. Grand Rapids: Zondervan, 2002.

Crisp, Oliver D. *Jonathan Edwards among the Theologians*. Grand Rapids: Eerdmans, 2015.

Culley, Robert C. "Psalm 88 among the Complaints." In *Ascribe to the Lord: Biblical and Other Studies in Memory of Peter C. Craigie*. Edited by Lyle Eslinger and Glen Taylor. *Journal for the Study of the Old Testament*. Supplement Series 67. Sheffield: Sheffield Academic, 1988.

Davis, John Jefferson. *Worship and the Reality of God: An Evangelical Theology of Real Presence*. Downers Grove, IL: InterVarsity, 2010.

Dobbs-Allsopp, F. W. *Weep, O Daughter of Zion: A Study of the City-Lament Genre in the Hebrew Bible*. Biblica Et Orientalia 44. Roma: Editrice Pontificio Istituto Biblico, 1993.

Duff, Nancy J. "Recovering Lamentation as a Practice in the Church." In *Lament: Reclaiming Practices in Pulpit, Pew, and Public Square*. Edited by Sally A. Brown and Patrick D. Miller. Louisville, KY: Westminster John Knox, 2005.

Dyson, Michael Eric. *Tears We Cannot Stop: A Sermon to White America*. New York: St. Martin's, 2017.

Ebner, Martin. "Klage und Auferweckungshoffnung im Neuen Testament." In *Klage, Jahrbuch für Biblische Theologie* 16. Neukirchen-Vluyn: Neukirchener, 2001.

Edwards, Jonathan. "The Dangers of Decline." In *Sermons and Discourses, 1730–1733*. Edited by Mark Valeri, 87–101. The Works of Jonathan Edwards 17. New Haven: Yale University Press, 1999.

Eklund, Rebekah. *Jesus Wept: The Significance of Jesus' Laments in the New Testament*. Library of New Testament Studies. London: Bloomsbury / T & T Clark, 2015.

Ellington, Scott A. *Risking Truth: Reshaping the World through Prayers of Lament*. Princeton Theological Monograph Series 98. Eugene, OR: Pickwick, 2008.

Emery, Giles. *Trinity, Church, and the Human Person: Thomistic Essays*. Faith & Reason: Studies in Catholic Theology & Philosophy. Naples, FL: Sapientia Press of Ave Maria University, 2007.

Estes, Daniel J. "The Transformation of Pain into Praise in the Individual Lament Psalms." In *The Psalms: Language for All Seasons of the Soul*. Edited by Andrew J. Schmutzer and David M. Howard Jr. Chicago: Moody, 2013.

Everhard, Matthew. "Interview with Robert Caldwell: Author of *Theologies of the American Revivalists*." *Jonathan Edward Studies*, May 24, 2017, https://edwardsstudies.com/2017/05/24/interview-with-robert-caldwell-author-of-theologies-of-the-american-revivalists/.

Farmer, Kathleen A. "Psalms." In *The Women's Bible Commentary*. Edited by Carol A. Newsom and Sharon H. Ringe. Louisville, KY: Westminster John Knox, 1992.

George, Timothy, ed. *Mr. Moody and the Evangelical Tradition*. London: T & T Clark, 2004.

Gerstenberger, Erhard S. *Psalms, Part 1 with an Introduction to Cultic Poetry*. Edited by Rolf Knierim and Gene M. Tucker. The Forms of the Old Testament Literature. Vol. 14. Grand Rapids: Eerdmans, 1988.

Goldingay, John. *Old Testament Theology, Volume 3: Israel's Life*. Downers Grove, IL: InterVarsity, 2009.

Green, Adam. "Reading the Mind of God (without Hebrew Lessons): Alston, Shared Attention, and Mystical Experience." *Religious Studies* 45, no. 4 (2009).

Guest, John. *The Communicator's Commentary: Jeremiah, Lamentations*. Waco, TX: Word Books, 1988.

Hall, Donald E. "Muscular Christianity: Reading and Writing the Male Social Body." In *Muscular Christianity: Embodying the Victorian Age*. Edited by Donald E. Hall, 3–13. Cambridge: Cambridge University Press, 1994.

Harper, G. Geoffrey, and Kit Barker, eds. *Finding Lost Words: The Church's Right to Lament*. Australian College of Theology Monograph Series. Eugene, OR: Wipf & Stock, 2017.

Harris, Murray J. *The Second Epistle to the Corinthians: A Commentary on the Greek Text*. The New International Greek Testament Commentary. Grand Rapids: Eerdmans, 2005.

Harrower, Scott. *God of All Comfort: A Trinitarian Response to the Horrors of This World*. Bellingham, WA: Lexham, 2019.

Hassler, Andrew. "Glimpses of Lament: 2 Corinthians and the Presence of Lament in the New Testament." *Journal of Spiritual Formation and Soul Care* 9, no. 2 (2016).

Hatch, Nathan O. *The Democratization of American Christianity*. New Haven: Yale University Press, 1989.

Hendrix, Scott H. *Recultivating the Vineyard: The Reformation Agendas of Christianization*. Louisville, KY: Westminster John Knox, 2004.

Hohenstein, Herbert E. "Oh Blessed Rage." *Current in Theology and Mission* 10, no. 3 (June 1983).

Hourdequin, Marion. "Empathy, Shared Intentionality, and Motivation by Moral Reasons." *Ethical Theory and Moral Practice* 15, no. 3 (2012).

Hughes, Richard A. "Lament, Death, and Destiny." *Society of Biblical Literature* 68. New York: Peter Lang, 2004.

Jenkins, Philip. *The Great and Holy War: How World War I Became a Religious Crusade*. New York: HarperOne, 2014.

Johnson, Luke Timothy. *The Letter of James*. Anchor Bible 37A. New York: Doubleday, 1995.

Jones, Serene. *Trauma and Grace: Theology in a Ruptured World*. Louisville, KY: Westminster John Knox, 2009.

Journet, Charles. *The Church of the Word Incarnate*. London: Sheed and Ward, 1955.

———. *Entretiens sur Dieu le Père*. Saint-Maur: Parole et silence, 1998.

———. *Entretiens sur l'espérance*. Saint-Maur: Parole et silence: Diffusion Cerf, 1998.

———. *Entretiens sur le Saint-Esprit*. Saint-Maur: Parole et Silence, 1997.

———. *The Mass: The Presence of the Sacrifice of the Cross*. South Bend, IN: St. Augustine's, 2008.

———. *The Theology of the Church*. San Francisco: Ignatius, 2004.
Journet, Charles, and Fondation Cardinal Journet. *Notre Père qui es aux cieux: retraite doctrinale*. Paris: Desclée de Brouwer, 1987.
Kelley, Page H. "Prayers of Troubled Saints." *Review & Expositor* 81 (1984).
Lee, Nancy C. *Lyrics of Lament: From Tragedy to Transformation*. Minneapolis: Fortress, 2010.
Longman III, Tremper. *How to Read the Psalms*. Downers Grove, IL: InterVarsity, 1988.
Marini, Stephen. "Hymnody as History: Early Evangelical Hymns and the Recovery of American Popular Religion." *Church History* 71, no. 2 (2002).
Miller, Robert J., Jacinta Ruru, Larissa Behrendt, and Tracey Lindberg. *Discovering Indigenous Lands: The Doctrine of Discovery in the English Colonies*. New York: Oxford University Press, 2010.
Miller, Robert J., and Elizabeth Forse. *Native America, Discovered and Conquered: Thomas Jefferson, Lewis & Clark, and Manifest Destiny*. Westport, CT: Praeger Publishers, 2006.
Morris, Thomas V. *The Logic of God Incarnate*. Ithaca, NY: Cornell University Press, 1986.
Morrow, William S. *Protest against God: The Eclipse of a Biblical Tradition*. Hebrew Bible Monographs 4. Sheffield: Sheffield Phoenix, 2006.
Murphy, Roland E. "The Last Truth about God." *Review & Expositor* 99 (2002).
O'Connor, Kathleen M. *Jeremiah: Pain and Promise*. Minneapolis: Fortress, 2012.
O'Day, Gail. "Surprised by Faith: Jesus and the Canaanite Woman." *Listening* 24 (1989).
Odell, Margaret S. "You Are What You Eat: Ezekiel and the Scroll Incident." *Journal of Biblical Literature* (January 1, 1998).
Öhler, Markus. "To Mourn, Weep, Lament, and Groan." *Evoking Lament: A Theological Discussion*. London: T & T Clark, 2009.
Okholm, Dennis L., ed. *The Gospel in Black & White: Theological Resources for Racial Reconciliation*. Downers Grove, IL: InterVarsity, 1997.

Pao, David, and Eckhard J. Schnabel. "Luke." In *Commentary on the New Testament Use of the Old Testament*. Edited by G. K. Beale and D. A. Carson. Grand Rapids: Baker, 2007.

Parry, Robin. "The Ethics of Lament: Lamentations 1 as a Case Study." In *Reading the Law: Essays in Honour of Gordon J. Wenham*. Edited by J. G. McConville and Karl Möller. The Library of Hebrew Bible/Old Testament Studies 461. London: T & T Clark, 2007.

Parry, Robin, ed. *Great Is Thy Faithfulness?: Reading Lamentations as Sacred Scripture*. Eugene, OR: Wipf & Stock, 2011.

Pemberton, Glenn. *After Lament: Psalms for Learning to Trust Again*. Abilene, TX: Abilene Christian University Press, 2014.

———. *Hurting with God: Learning to Lament with the Psalms*. Abilene, TX: Abilene Christian University Press, 2012.

Peterson, David. *Engaging with God: A Biblical Theology of Worship*. Downers Grove, IL: InterVarsity, 1992.

Petter, Donna Lee. *The Book of Ezekiel and Mesopotamian City Laments*. Orbis Biblicus Et Orientalis. Fribourg: Academic, 2011.

———. "Notes on Ezekiel." *NIV Zondervan Study Bible: New International Version*. Edited by D. A. Carson. Grand Rapids: Zondervan, 2015.

Phillips, John. *Exploring the Gospel of John: An Expository Commentary*. Grand Rapids: Kregel Publications, 1989.

Pinn, Anthony B. *The Black Church in the Post-Civil Rights Era*. Maryknoll, NY: Orbis Books, 2002.

Pinsent, Andrew. *The Second-Person Perspective in Aquinas's Ethics: Virtues and Gifts*. Routledge Studies in Ethics and Moral Theory 17. New York: Routledge, 2012.

Price III, Emmett G., ed. *The Black Church and Hip Hop Culture: Toward Bridging the Generational Divide*. Lanham, MD: Scarecrow, 2012.

Raboteau, Albert J. *Slave Religion: The "Invisible Institution" in the Antebellum South*. New York: Oxford University Press, 1978.

Rah, Soong-Chan. *Prophetic Lament: A Call for Justice in Troubled Times*. Downers Grove, IL: InterVarsity, 2015.

Rambo, Shelly. "Spirit and Trauma." *Interpretation: A Journal of Bible and Theology* 69, no. 1 (2014).

Rindge, Matthew. "Reconfiguring the Akedah and Recasting God: Lament and Divine Abandonment in Mark." In *Journal of Biblical Literature* 130, no. 1 (2011).
Saliers, Don E. *Worship Come To Its Senses*. Nashville: Abingdon, 1996.
Sanders, Jack T. *The New Testament Christological Hymns*. Cambridge: Cambridge University Press, 2004.
Schaefer, Charles A., and Frauke C. Schaefer, eds. *Trauma and Resilience: A Handbook*. N.p.: Frauke C. Shaefer, MD, Inc., 2012.
Schwanda, Tom, ed. *The Emergence of Evangelical Spirituality: The Age of Edwards, Newton, and Whitefield*. The Classics of Western Spirituality. New York: Paulist, 2016.
Schwindt, Rainer. "Der Klageruf der Märtyer." In *Biblische Notizen*, NF 141 and NF 142 (2009).
Seow, Choon-Leong. "Job." *Dictionary of Scripture and Ethics*. Edited by Joel B. Green. Grand Rapids: Baker, 2011.
Simundson, Daniel J. *Faith under Fire: Biblical Interpretations of Suffering*. Minneapolis: Augsburg, 1980.
———. *The Message of Job: A Theological Commentary*. Augsburg OT Studies. Minneapolis: Augsburg, 1986.
Sittser, Jerry L. *A Grace Disguised: How the Soul Grows through Loss*. Grand Rapids: Zondervan, 1996.
Sloane, Andrew. "Lament and the Journey of Doubt." *Christian Scholar's Review* 29, no. 1 (1999).
Starling, David. "'For Your Sake We Are Being Killed All Day Long': Romans 8:36 and the Hermeneutics of Unexplained Suffering." *Themelios* 42, no. 1 (2017).
Stump, Eleonore. "Atonement and the Cry of Dereliction from the Cross." *European Journal for Philosophy of Religion* 4, no. 1 (2012).
———. "Narrative and the Knowledge of Persons." *Euresis Journal* 5 (2013).
———. *Wandering in Darkness: Narrative and the Problem of Suffering*. Oxford: Oxford University Press, 2010.
Sutton, Matthew Avery. *American Apocalypse: A History of Modern Evangelicalism*. Cambridge, MA: The Belknap Press of Harvard University Press, 2014.

Thomas, Heath. *Poetry and Theology in the Book of Lamentations: The Aesthetics of an Open Text.* Hebrew Bible Monographs. Sheffield: Sheffield Phoenix, 2013.

———. "Suffering." *Dictionary of the Old Testament: Prophets.* Edited by Mark J. Boda and J. Gordon McConville. IVP Bible Dictionary. Downers Grove, IL: IVP Academic, 2012.

Tutu, Desmond. Quoted in Gustavo Gutiérrez, *On Job: God-Talk and the Suffering of the Innocent.* Translated by Matthew J. O'Connell. Maryknoll: Orbis, 1987.

Tyson, Timothy B. *The Blood of Emmett Till.* New York: Simon & Schuster, 2017.

Villanueva, Federico G. *"The Uncertainty of a Hearing": A Study of the Sudden Change of Mood in the Lament Psalms.* Leiden: Brill, 2008.

Villanueva, Rico G. *It's OK to Be Not OK: The Message of the Lament Psalms.* Manila: OMF Literature, 2012.

von Rad, Gerhard. *The Message of the Prophets.* New York: Harper & Row, 1965.

Wacker, Grant. *America's Pastor: Billy Graham and the Shaping of a Nation.* Cambridge, MA: The Belknap Press of Harvard University Press, 2014.

Ward, W. Reginald. *The Protestant Evangelical Awakening.* Cambridge: Cambridge University Press, 1992.

Ware, Bruce A. "The Man Christ Jesus." *Journal of the Evangelical Theological Society* 53, no. 1 (2010).

Warfield, Benjamin Breckinridge. *The Person and Work of Christ.* Phillipsburg, NJ: Presbyterian and Reformed, 1950.

Washington Jr., Joseph R. *Black Religion: The Negro and Christianity in the United States.* Boston: Beacon, 1964.

West, Cornel. *Black Prophetic Fire.* Boston: Beacon, 2014.

Westermann, Claus. *Elements of Old Testament Theology.* Translated by Douglas W. Scott. Louisville, KY: John Knox, 1982.

———. "The Role of the Lament in the Theology of the Old Testament." In *Interpretation* 28 (1974).

———. *The Structure of the Book of Job: A Form-Critical Analysis.* Translated by C. A. Muenchow. Philadelphia: Fortress, 1977.

White, James F. *A Brief History of Christian Worship*. Nashville: Abingdon, 1993.

Wilson, Gerald Henry. *The Editing of the Hebrew Psalter*. Society of Biblical Literature Dissertation Series 76. Chico, CA: Scholars, 1985.

Wolterstorff, Nicholas. "The Art of Lament." The Banner. July 27, 2012. http://www.thebanner.org.

Zahavi, D. "You, Me, and We: The Sharing of Emotional Experience." *Journal of Consciousness Studies* 22, no. 1–2 (2015).

# Contributors

**Rhys S. Bezzant** (ThD, Australian College of Theology) is an ordained Anglican and lecturer in church history at Ridley College in Melbourne, Australia. He is the director of the Jonathan Edwards Center Australia, a Visiting Fellow at Yale Divinity School, and the canon of St. Paul's Cathedral in Melbourne. He is also the author of *Jonathan Edwards and the Church* (Oxford University Press, 2014), *Standing on their Shoulders* (Acorn, 2015), *Edwards the Mentor* (Oxford University Press, 2019), and the translator of *Martin Luther: A Late Medieval* Life (Baker, 2017).

**Scott Harrower** (PhD, Trinity International University) is a lecturer in Christian thought at Ridley College in Melbourne, Australia. An ordained Anglican minister, Scott has worked in medical trauma rooms and has a long history of involvement in spiritual formation and retreat ministries, specializing in trauma and recovery. He is the author of *God of All Comfort: A Trinitarian Response to the Horrors of This World* (Faithlife, 2019).

**Sean M. McDonough** (PhD, University of St. Andrews) is professor of New Testament at Gordon-Conwell Theological Seminary in South Hamilton, Massachusetts. His books include *Creation and New Creation* (Hendrickson, 2016), *Christ as Creator* (Oxford University Press, 2010) and *YHWH at Patmos* (Mohr Siebeck, 1999). He is active as a teacher and preacher at First Congregational Church of Hamilton, Massachusetts.

**Donna Petter** (PhD, University of Toronto) is director of the Hebrew Language Program and associate professor of Old Testament at Gordon-Conwell Theological Seminary. She is a contributor to the *Baker Illustrated Bible Commentary* (2012) and the *NIV Zondervan Study Bible* (2015), and author of *The Book of Ezekiel and Mesopotamian City Laments* (Vandenhoeck & Ruprecht, 2011). She is coauthor with her husband and colleague, Tom Petter, of a commentary on *Ezra-Nehemiah* in the New International Version Application Commentary Series (Zondervan, 2019). She is also currently writing a commentary on Ezekiel. An ordained Congregational minister, Donna has served in various capacities at Trinitarian Congregational Church of Wayland, Massachusetts.

**Emmett G. Price III** (PhD, University of Pittsburgh) is professor of worship, church & culture, dean of the chapel (Hamilton Campus), and founding executive director of the Institute for the Study of the Black Christian Experience (ISBCE) at Gordon-Conwell Theological Seminary. He is the executive editor of the *Encyclopedia of African American Music* (ABC-CLIO, 2011), and editor of *The Black Church and Hip Hop Culture: Toward Bridging the Generational Divide* (Scarecrow Press, 2012). He is the founding pastor of Community of Love Christian Fellowship in Boston.

**Lindsay Wilson** (PhD, Melbourne) is senior lecturer in Old Testament at Ridley College, Melbourne. He is the author of commentaries on *Job* (Two Horizons, 2015) and *Proverbs* (Tyndale, 2017), as well as *Joseph Wise and Otherwise* (Paternoster, 2004). He is an ordained Anglican minister who is also active in training theological educators and preachers in South and Southeast Asia.